SUPER SIMPLE
OUTDOOR
WOODWORKING

SUPER SIMPLE
OUTDOOR
WOODWORKING

15 PRACTICAL WEEKEND PROJECTS

RANDALL A. MAXEY

Contents

Introduction

My goal in writing this book was to design easy-to-build outdoor furniture projects that you can make using just a few simple tools and commonly available lumber from a home center. You will find a variety of projects that make wonderful additions to your landscape.

For these projects, it doesn't matter if you have any woodworking experience. With this book in hand, you will discover that building attention-getting projects for your outdoor landscape or garden space is an enjoyable endeavor. Just follow the step-by-step instructions—along with the photos and illustrations—for guaranteed success. You don't need a spacious workshop full of big, expensive power tools. Your tool kit need not be much more than a saw and power drill. Your backyard is your workshop.

Not only did I set out to design simple furniture, but my aim was also to make the projects practical. For example, I designed the swing, chair, and seating bench so they would be comfortable to sit in for extended periods of time. For each of these

projects, the seat and back are angled for comfort. This means that careful attention to detail is in order when measuring and marking the pieces for cutting and assembly. Some pieces require angled cuts, and some assemblies involve angles when fastening them together. Following the instructions for each step makes the process easy, manageable, and straightforward.

You will find that some projects are designed for you to build in a few hours. For these, most of the parts involve square cuts assembled with screws. You'll be surprised at how quickly the projects come together. Other projects require a little more study of the photos and illustrations before you start building, and some require an extra pair of hands for assembly. In all cases, you will find that woodworking, especially when building outdoor projects, is more enjoyable in the company of a friend or neighbor.

So, head to the home center to purchase the lumber you need, gather up your tools, then get outside to start building your *Super Simple Outdoor Woodworking* project. What are you waiting for?

Tools and Techniques

The selection of tools you need to build any of the projects in this book is minimal. A few hand tools and a battery-powered or electric drill will get the job done. If you have access to power tools like a circular saw or miter saw, they will make the job go quicker.

1 Handsaw
2 Power drill
3 Circular saw
4 Spade (paddle) drill bits
5 Exterior-grade screws
6 Exterior-grade hardware
7 Carpenter's square
8 Tape measure
9 Drill and countersink bits
10 Driver bit

Basic tools are all you need to make great projects you can be proud of.

TOOLS REQUIRED

Circular saw or miter saw (handsaw can also be used)
Handsaw
Screwdriver (or electric drill)
#8 countersink bit (to avoid splitting)
Electric drill
Straightedge (yardstick)
Tape measure

Combination square
Carpenter's square
Spade (paddle) drill bits
Basic set of twist drill bits
Sander
Work surface or workbench

SAFETY

1 Earmuffs
2 Dust mask
3 Ear plugs
4 Safety glasses

Safety gear is a must-have when using power tools for woodworking.

Woodworking with hand tools requires a little care and common sense. For example, when using a saw, make sure the blade will not make contact with your fingers during the cut. Another thing to watch for when using a handsaw or circular saw is to avoid cutting into your work surface. It happens to the best of us but only when we don't check to see where the saw is positioned before we start the cut.

When using a power tool of any sort, be sure to wear eye protection. Flying sawdust and wood chips are a nuisance but wearing inexpensive safety glasses or goggles is insurance against potential eye injury.

Another must-have accessory when using loud power tools, such as circular saws or miter saws, is hearing protection. You can buy inexpensive foam or silicone

earplugs from a home center. Look for a noise reduction rating (NRR) of 20 or greater for the best hearing protection. If you use earplugs, be sure to follow the instructions to get a good fit in your ears to block out damaging noise.

Over-the-ear earmuffs provide an excellent option for hearing protection. Some folks find them more comfortable than earplugs. The choice is yours, but don't start up any loud power tools without some form of hearing protection.

Finally, sawing wood generates a lot of sawdust, so it's a good idea to wear a dust mask. The disposable masks are inexpensive and do a good job of preventing fine dust particles from entering the lungs.

You may already have a tape measure in your tool kit. Use a gel pen instead of a pencil to make your layout lines stand out.

A plastic carpenter's square is one of the handiest tools you can own. It's ideal for marking, for use as a saw guide, and for squaring up project assemblies.

The tools you need to mark the cut lines on the wood are basic. A tape measure with a pen or pencil come into play on every board for each of the projects. Use a pencil with a sharp point to make clear and legible lines. Use inexpensive mechanical pencils to avoid sharpening. To make the marks and layout lines more visible, a gel pen with black ink does a great job.

CARPENTER'S SQUARE

One tool I find indispensable for projects is a carpenter's square. It's sometimes called a "speed square" or "rafter square." Available in metal and plastic versions, they are ideal for marking square and miter (45°) cuts. I prefer the plastic version because they are so inexpensive, and I don't have to worry about damaging the edge of a tool upon accidental contact with the square. You can find carpenter's squares about 7 or 8in (180 or 200mm) long or in a larger 12in (305mm) size. I keep both sizes on hand. The larger square is handy for squaring up project parts during project assembly.

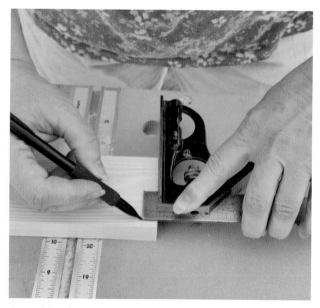

A combination square is great for marking off distances from the edge of a workpiece. A practical example is marking locations for screws.

YARDSTICK OR METERSTICK

Another tool you may find handy is a yardstick or meterstick. Made of wood or aluminum, these are great as a straightedge for marking lines. The measuring scale is an added bonus for layout work.

COMBINATION SQUARE

One tool that many serious woodworkers have at their disposal is a combination square. It consists of a metal rule that slides in a metal head. By loosening the knob in the square's head, you can slide the rule until it projects from the head the desired amount then tighten the knob to secure it.

A combination square is one of those tools you will use often, so it pays to buy a quality one. I look for rules that have inked or etched markings. The markings should be crisp and easy to read and the rule should be simple to adjust. Stay away from squares that have a stamped rule. They tend to be less accurate, hard to adjust, and will only frustrate you in the end.

SAWING

An inexpensive handsaw does a great job of cutting parts to length. Look for one designed for crosscutting.

The one tool you'll use most, other than a screwdriver, is a saw. Every part needs to be cut to final length before assembling the project. There is a variety of ways to cut a board to length: a handsaw, circular saw, or miter saw. The least expensive and most readily available is a handsaw. You can find them at home centers. A common length is around 15in (380mm).

HANDSAW

One thing to bear in mind when shopping for handsaws is the tooth count, or number of teeth per inch (TPI). Tooth counts less than 10TPI are designed to make rough cuts and can cause splintering, or tearout, along the cut edge. For smoother cuts with less splintering, choose a saw with 10TPI or more.

Using a handsaw takes a little practice but becomes second nature after a while. Start the cut at the edge farthest away from you and cut toward your body. The hardest part of using a handsaw is starting the cut. The

saw tends to skip away from the cut line. To avoid this, position the saw next to the cut line and place the end of the thumb of your free hand against the blade above the teeth. Your thumb acts as a stop to keep the saw on track for the first few strokes. Don't force the saw or apply downward pressure—let the weight of the saw do the work. Make a few strokes until you start cutting a groove, called a "saw kerf." Once the groove is deep enough, you can pull your free hand away from the saw to support the workpiece. Start making longer strokes, keeping an eye on the cut line. If you can, support the cutoff piece through the last stroke to prevent it from dropping before the cut is finished. Doing so results in a smoother cut without splitting that can occur if the piece falls free before the cut is complete.

CIRCULAR SAW

If you have access to a circular saw, either battery-powered or cordless, it will make cutting parts to size much easier and quicker. You don't need a large

A circular saw makes quick work of cutting workpieces to final size.

Miter saws are the ultimate tool for cutting parts to length.

saw—a small trim saw will do the job nicely and is easier to handle.

Like a handsaw, or any saw for that matter, the more teeth there are on the blade, the smoother the cut. Some stock blades that come with the saw are designed for rough cuts on construction lumber. You might consider buying a better replacement blade with more teeth for smoother cuts.

If you're experienced with a circular saw, you can certainly follow a straight cut line freehand, without the aid of a guide. However, it can be beneficial to use a straightedge guide to get consistently straight and square cuts every time. A carpenter's square works great as a saw guide, as shown in the photo above right. Simply line the saw blade up at the edge of the workpiece adjacent to the cut line, then slide the square tight against the saw's base, making sure the fence of the square is tight against the edge of the workpiece. Now you can make the cut, keeping the saw against the edge of the square throughout the cut.

MITER SAW

Perhaps the quickest and most accurate tool for cutting project parts to length is a miter saw. Larger miter saws

can be hard on the budget but, fortunately, you can get by with the smallest of miter saws (some are battery-powered) for most cuts on your projects. Plus, you're sure to find other uses for it in the future. Consider it an investment in your woodworking tool arsenal.

Miter saws have advantages besides their convenience. First, they have a long fence that helps register the workpiece for a square cut. With the blade raised, it's important to make sure the workpiece has contact with the fence on either side of the blade. Otherwise, the cut will not be square. Another benefit of a miter saw is speed. With a miter saw you can quickly and more easily cut parts than using a handsaw or circular saw. For projects with many parts, you can get into "production mode" and cut several parts before assembling them in your project.

When it comes time to make angled cuts, a miter saw excels at that, as well. All you need to do is pivot the saw carriage and table to the desired angle and make the cut as you would a square cut. (Read the owner's manual for the proper procedure for your saw.) Some more advanced miter saws also offer the ability to tilt the blade in relation to the table, enabling you to make compound angle cuts. That functionality isn't required for the projects in this book.

DRILLING AND DRIVING

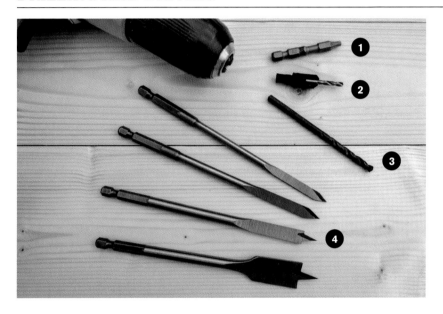

1 Driver bit
2 Countersink bit
3 Twist drill bit
4 Spade (paddle) drill bits

Spade (paddle) drill bits and standard twist drill bits are handy to have in your toolbox. Keep an assortment of driver bits on hand for driving screws.

Drilling holes in wood may seem simple, but there are some tips and techniques you can use to get professional results.

TWIST DRILL BITS

For the projects in this book, a basic set of twist drill bits is all that is required. These are the standard drill bits you find in the hardware store. Purchase a set of 8–12 bits. A small set provides enough variety for the holes needed for the projects.

One of the problems you may encounter when drilling through wood is tearout or chipping on the back side of the workpiece as the bit exits the wood. With standard twist drill bits, taking it slow and easy as the bit approaches the opposite side of the workpiece helps minimize tearout. Another option is to clamp a scrap piece of wood to the back side of the workpiece

Use a twist drill bit to create a shank, or clearance, hole for screw threads.

Spade bits chew through wood quickly to create larger holes than those you could drill with commonly available twist bits.

To leave a clean hole with minimal tearout and chipping when using a spade bit, drill from both sides of the workpiece.

where the hole will exit. This helps support the wood fibers to leave a clean hole with crisp edges.

SPADE (PADDLE) DRILL BITS

Another style of bits for your toolbox are spade bits, sometimes called paddle bits. These inexpensive bits excel at drilling larger holes quickly. Here, a set of bits with sizes ranging from ¼in to 1½in (6.5mm to 38mm) would make a versatile selection for most tasks.

There's a trick you can use with spade bits that minimizes tearout. As you drill through the workpiece, stop drilling as soon as you see the center point of the bit poke through the opposite side. Then drill from the opposite side, using the small hole as a guide to center the drill bit.

SCREWS

To assemble most of the projects in this book, you'll be using flathead wood screws. And lots of them. A portable electric or battery-powered hand drill is your friend here. Other than driving screws, there are quite a few holes to drill, so a selection of drill bits is good to have.

Since these projects will be used outdoors, look for screws that are rated for exterior use. Most have a coating to help prevent rust.

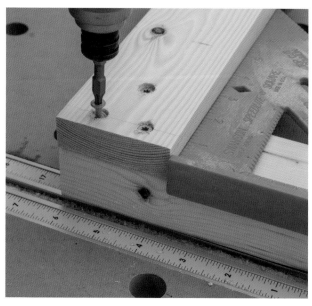

By predrilling holes for screws, you avoid splitting the wood and end up with a neater assembly.

TIP
When using any kind of drill bit on wood, take it slow and let the drill bit do the work. A sharp drill bit should cut cleanly and easily without you having to apply pressure. For deep holes, sawdust can get compacted within the hole and cause the bit to quit cutting. Withdraw the bit from the hole periodically as you're drilling to remove sawdust and chips.

As you are probably aware, screws come in dozens of sizes and varieties. They are rated first by their diameter expressed as a number, for example, a #8 (4mm), and this is the diameter that you'll be mostly using for these projects. After the diameter classification comes the length of the screw. The length depends on the fastening requirements, but common lengths used here are 1¼in (30mm), 1½in (40mm), 2in (50mm), and 2½in (60mm). You'll see on the package of screws the diameter designation followed by the length: #8 x 1¼in (4 x 30mm), for example.

Screws used for construction have a self-drilling point that, in theory, eliminates the need to predrill a pilot hole for the screw. However, if you drive a screw near the end of the board on softwood like pine, the tapered screw head may split the wood. To get around this, use a countersink bit to predrill a hole. You can find countersink bits at a home center or hardware store. They feature a drill bit housed in a larger steel bit that forms the tapered hole for the screw head.

As you drive a screw to fasten two pieces together, sometimes the threads on the screw will "jack up" the top piece as it contacts the lower piece. If this becomes a problem, follow up the countersink bit with a standard drill bit with the same, or slightly larger, diameter as the thread diameter on the screw. Drill through the top piece only. Doing this allows the threads to slip though the workpiece without grabbing while the screwhead tightens the joint. It's a good idea to practice on some scrap pieces first to see if this step is necessary.

Many screw manufacturers include a driver bit sized to fit the screw. This fits in your electric drill or driver to drive the screws. I find it easier to use a set of longer driver bits. Just make sure they're the right size to fit the head of the screw. When driving the screw with a power drill, it's easy to overdrive it, which can cause splitting. Instead, take it easy and just snug up the joint and call it done.

Construction screws feature a self-drilling tip and coarse threads to securely fasten softwoods.

From left to right are shown a typical wood screw used for exterior construction; a Torx driver bit to fit the head of the screw; a standard twist drill bit for predrilling a shank hole for the screw; and a countersink bit.

TIP
On some project assemblies, you may find it difficult to fit the drill and driver into the space above the screw to drive it home. If you don't have access to a smaller power driver, a short, old-fashioned screwdriver can do the job.

SANDING

Sandpaper wrapped around a wood cutoff makes a handy sanding block for smoothing edges and surfaces of your projects.

After the project is assembled, there's one more important step before you can call it a day. Woodworking almost always involves a certain amount of sanding to remove splinters, smooth surfaces, and round over sharp corners. To do this, you need nothing more than sheets of sandpaper and a block of wood. Wrap the sandpaper around the wood block to form a firm, flat surface for the sandpaper. Soften all the sharp edges and smooth the surfaces.

To make the job go quicker, use an electric or battery-powered random orbital sander. It makes sanding less tedious and eliminates the need for the elbow grease required for sanding by hand.

When shopping for sandpaper, look for 100- or 120-grit. This grit cuts efficiently, especially on softwoods, and results in a smooth surface.

WOOD AND FINISHES

Softwoods are the most common species at a home center.

The projects here are designed to be built from lumber that you can find at a home center. In some areas, this limits your choices of the type of wood. Spruce, pine, and fir are species used in construction lumber. You'll find a selection of boards for projects in these species, as well. If other species, like hardwoods, are available where you shop, you can make the choice which to use based on your budget.

Since you've put some effort into building your outdoor project, there are some things you can do to keep it looking great. If you can minimize exposure to direct sunlight and moisture, you're ahead of the game. If a project is destined to set directly on soil, using small pavers to keep it elevated off the ground allows air to circulate, prolonging the life of the wood. If the project is portable, during winter months consider covering it with a waterproof tarp, storing it in a shed, under an awning, or in a garage to keep it dry. If fallen leaves are common in your neighborhood, they trap moisture if allowed to accumulate on wood, contributing to staining, mold, and decay.

Before you start building your project, consider whether you want to apply a finish or paint to protect it from the elements. A protective finish rated for exterior projects is formulated to protect against moisture and harmful ultraviolet (UV) rays from the sun. Bare wood that is left exposed will deteriorate more quickly without an application of a quality finish. Your choices of finish vary depending on the look you're after, its ease of application and of upkeep. The first, and perhaps most popular for outdoor projects, is an oil stain.

A NOTE ABOUT LUMBER SIZES

When lumber is processed at a sawmill, the mill will cut the logs into boards of rough dimensions. For example, a 2x4 will be close to actual 2 x 4in (50 x 100mm) dimensions. The lumber then goes into a kiln to remove most of the moisture. Once the lumber is dried to industry-standard moisture content, it is milled to final size before transport to your local retailer. For example, the 2x4 will be trimmed and thicknessed down to an actual size of 1½ x 3½in (38 x 90mm). One thing to be aware of, however, is that most retailers still label the product by its nominal size. So, a board labeled "2 x 4in" will actually measure 1½ x 3½in (38 x 90mm). For the projects in this book, we'll be showing and using the actual dimensions of the lumber in the materials lists and instructions. Below is a chart you can use when shopping for lumber to help you understand what you need versus what you're buying.

LUMBER DIMENSIONS

ACTUAL MEASUREMENT	NOMINAL MEASUREMENT
¾ x 1½in (19 x 38mm)	1 x 2in (25 x 50mm)
¾ x 2½in (19 x 63mm)	1 x 3in (25 x 75mm)
¾ x 3½in (19 x 90mm)	1 x 4in (25 x 100mm)
¾ x 5½in (19 x 140mm)	1 x 6in (25 x 150mm)
1½ x 1½in (38 x 38mm)	2 x 2 (50 x 50mm)
1½ x 2½in (38 x 63mm)	2 x 3 (50 x 75mm)
1½ x 3½in (38 x 90mm)	2 x 4 (50 x 100mm)
1½ x 5½in (38 x 140mm)	2 x 6 (50 x 150mm)
3½ x 3½in (90 x 90mm)	4 x 4 (100 x 100mm)

Exterior stains add protection and a bit of color to your project.

Use a good-quality exterior paint to add a splash of color.

STAIN

One option for a finish is an exterior stain like one you would use on a porch or deck surface. Oil stains come in a variety of colors as well as clear. The colors in a stain are somewhat transparent—not opaque as in a painted finish.

Oil stains are easy to apply with a brush or small roller. The stain soaks into the wood fibers, providing extra protection against sunlight and moisture. Because a stain doesn't form a cured film on the surface of the wood as paint does, you can easily renew it by applying a new coat every year or two, depending on the manufacturer's recommendations. Doing this regularly extends the life of the wood.

PAINT

If you're after a splash of color for your project, paint provides a vast array of color choices. As with a stain, use a paint rated for exterior use. The pigments and resins used in exterior coatings minimize color fading with constant exposure to direct sunlight.

For the best results and a longer-lasting finish, apply a quality, exterior-grade primer to the bare wood before applying the color coats. The primer's job is to seal the wood and provide a surface for the paint that aids adhesion, preventing peeling.

Unlike an oil finish that soaks into the wood fibers, paint forms what is known as a film finish. The idea is that a consistent film of paint adds a barrier against moisture and sunlight.

There are a couple of things to think about before you get out the paintbrush. A painted finish relies on an unbroken film to protect the wood. Wood, by nature, expands and contracts with changes in humidity and temperature. Eventually, this continuous, inflexible paint barrier becomes compromised and cracks. This allows moisture to migrate under the paint layer, which causes peeling. Keeping a painted finish looking good requires a little maintenance.

A painted finish can't be renewed as with an oil finish. The only solution is to scrape off any peeling paint and thoroughly sand the project before applying a new coat of paint. Now, before you get discouraged about the possibility of using paint, know that a quality exterior paint should last for years before you need to add another coat.

Apply an exterior-grade or marine-grade varnish to provide a tough, protective film on your project.

Apply finish to each component of your project before assembly for the ultimate protection against moisture.

MARINE VARNISH OR EPOXY

The last classification of finishes includes a marine varnish and epoxy. Marine varnish, sometimes called spar varnish, was originally formulated as a finish for the spar (mast) in a sailing vessel. As the name implies, a marine varnish is formulated to protect wood used in boats. So, you know it's got to be tough and stand up to harsh environments.

There are many varieties of marine varnish and choosing one can be difficult. Rely on the expertise of a paint store or marine supply store to help you out. Not only can they help you choose the right finish, but they also advise on how to apply it and get the best results. Do your research and ask a lot of questions before making your decision. Marine varnishes can be more expensive and more difficult to apply than other types of finish.

Epoxy is a two-part finish that forms a thick, hard coating that stands up to a lot of abuse. It's what many restaurants use to protect the wood on their tabletops. Epoxy consists of a resin component and a catalyst that, when blended in very precise amounts, chemically react to fully cure the finish. Using epoxy requires some practice and special equipment to mix and apply the finish. It's also costly to purchase. I wouldn't recommend using epoxy unless you have experience with it. If you decide you want to give epoxy a try, check with a marine supplier to get advice on what to use and gain some tips for applying it.

PREFINISHING

No matter what finish you choose, consider prefinishing the parts of your project before final assembly. This may not be practical for every project but applying finish to each part beforehand provides the best protection, especially on assembled joints where two parts are fastened together. Your goal is to minimize water penetration to bare wood. Water tends to wick into joints where it is trapped.

You can cut and drill most parts then apply a finish. Then all you need to do is assemble the project and not have to deal with applying a finish to the entire project all at once.

These tips and tricks will go a long way to helping you get the results on your project that you can be proud of. Let's get started!

Side Table

Whether you're entertaining guests or just relaxing in the sunshine, this side table comes in handy as a place to set drinks, books, or snacks. Build one or several to provide some flexibility in your outdoor furniture layouts. A quick build, this small table provides a great opportunity to practice basic woodworking skills.

Lumber required
1   1½ x 2½ x 96in (38 x 63 x 2440mm)
1   ¾ x 3½ x 96in (19 x 90 x 2440mm)
1   ¾ x 2½ x 96in (19 x 63 x 2440mm)
1   1½ x 1½ x 96in (38 x 38 x 2440mm)

Materials required
1lb (454g) #8 x 1¼in (4 x 30mm) exterior screws
1lb (454g) #8 x 2in (4 x 50mm) exterior screws

OVERALL DIMENSIONS

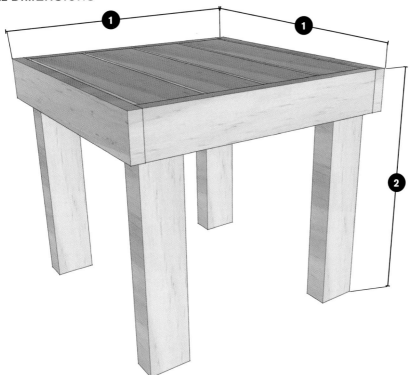

1 16¾in (424mm)
2 14¾in (374mm)

MAKING THE TOP FRAME

1 16¾in (424mm)
2 15¼in (386mm)

1 The top frame of the table forms the basis for the rest of the construction. Start by cutting the four pieces for the top frame of the table from ¾ x 2½in (19 x 63mm) stock. Note that the lengths of the two pairs that make up the frame are different. One pair is 1½in (38mm) shorter. This ensures that the overall dimension of the finished top is square.

2 A miter saw makes quick work of cutting parts to length, but you could also use a circular saw or handsaw. After you have the four frame parts cut, set them aside while you cut the legs. They're made from 1½ x 2½in (38 x 63mm) boards. Then you can start building the leg assemblies and finish the top frame.

3 You'll be building two leg assemblies connected by the remaining pieces of the top frame. Note that the top frame projects ¾in (19mm) above the top of the legs. The slats that make up the tabletop sit inside and flush with the top of the frame.

TIP
While you have the saw set up, cut the four pieces that make up the slats of the tabletop and set them aside. Cut them 15¼in (386mm) long from a ¾ x 3½in (19 x 90mm) board.

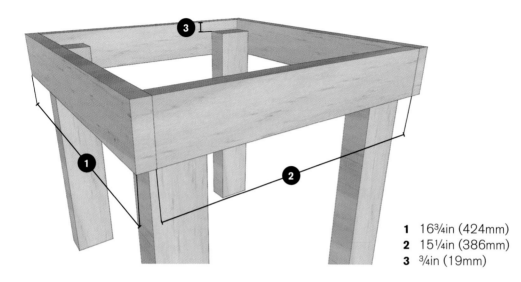

1   16¾in (424mm)
2   15¼in (386mm)
3   ¾in (19mm)

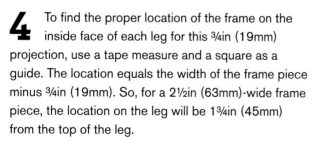

4 To find the proper location of the frame on the inside face of each leg for this ¾in (19mm) projection, use a tape measure and a square as a guide. The location equals the width of the frame piece minus ¾in (19mm). So, for a 2½in (63mm)-wide frame piece, the location on the leg will be 1¾in (45mm) from the top of the leg.

5 Mark the location on each leg with a line. Use this line as a reference to locate the bottom of the frame when attaching it to the inside of the legs. It also helps locate the frame pieces to create a ¾in (19mm) recess in the top for the slats.

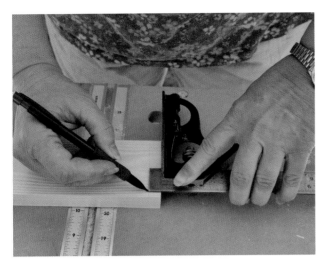

6 Before assembling the base of the table, I like to predrill the screw holes in the four frame pieces before fastening the frame to the legs. To get consistent spacing for a professional look, mark the screw locations on the workpieces before drilling. A combination square is an ideal tool for this, but you can just as easily use a tape measure or ruler. To mark locations for the screws that secure the frame to the legs, measure ⅜in (10mm) from the end of the top frame pieces and mark a line. Here, using a pencil makes it easier to sand away the lines later.

7 To locate the screw holes a consistent distance from the edges, make a mark at 1in (25mm) that crosses the line you made earlier. Where these marks cross is where you will predrill for the screws.

8 Use a countersink drill bit followed by a twist drill bit to provide clearance for the screw threads. Using the technique for predrilling screw holes shown in Chapter 1 (see page 14) helps prevent the wood from splitting as you tighten the screw. Because the shorter frame pieces are fastened to the wide face of the legs, you can add a third screw location for additional strength.

9 Now you can lay out a pair of table legs and connect them with one of the shorter frame pieces. Use a square to align the frame piece flush with the outside edge. Use the lines you marked on the legs to position the bottom of the frame piece. The frame should extend ¾in (19mm) above the top of the leg. Use 2in (50mm) screws to fasten the shorter frame piece to the legs, making sure it's square to the legs.

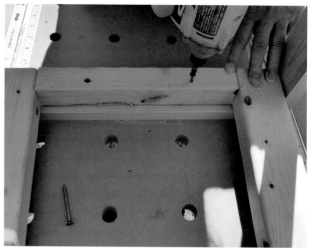

10 Connect the two leg assemblies with the longer frame pieces, keeping the outside edges flush. Note that the frame projects ¾in (19mm) above the legs.

11 There are two more pieces to add to the frame before you set it upright to add the slats. These are the cleats that fit between the legs to support the slats. Cut these from 1 ½ x 1 ½in (38 x 38mm) stock to fit between two legs and fasten them with 2in (50mm) screws from the inside, as shown in the photo.

12 At last, you can set the table up on all four legs and loosely set the slats in place with the ends resting on the top of the legs and cleats. With the slats in place, you're on the homestretch to a completed table.

13 The final task is to fasten the slats in place with screws. Again, for a consistent, professional look, take the time to locate and drill each screw hole. A combination square comes in handy for marking screw locations from the ends of the slats. Locate this line approximately ¾in (19mm) from the ends of the slats.

14 Mark 1 in (25mm) from the edges of the slats to locate the screw hole locations. Remove the slats and predrill the screw holes as before. Put them back in place and take a moment to space them so the overall top is pleasing to your eye. Then you can drive the screws to fix them in place.

15 Visually space the slats before fastening them in place with 1¼in (30mm) screws. The only thing left to do now is decide where you're going to place the table. Hopefully, it's in a spot where you can kick back and relax with a good book, a tall beverage, and a tasty snack.

Garden Bridge

Decorative, but also functional, this garden bridge can span a small fountain stream or a stream of gravel. It adds a focal point to your landscape while making your backyard retreat appear larger. Building this garden bridge is a fun project, especially if you have a helper.

LUMBER REQUIRED

3   2 x 3 x 96in (50 x 75 x 2440mm)
5   1 x 4 x 96in (25 x 100 x 2440mm)
3   1 x 6 x 96in (25 x 150 x 2440mm)

MATERIALS REQUIRED

1lb (454g) #8 x 1¼in (4 x 30mm) exterior
   screws
1lb (454g) #8 x 2in (4 x 50mm) exterior screws

OVERALL DIMENSIONS

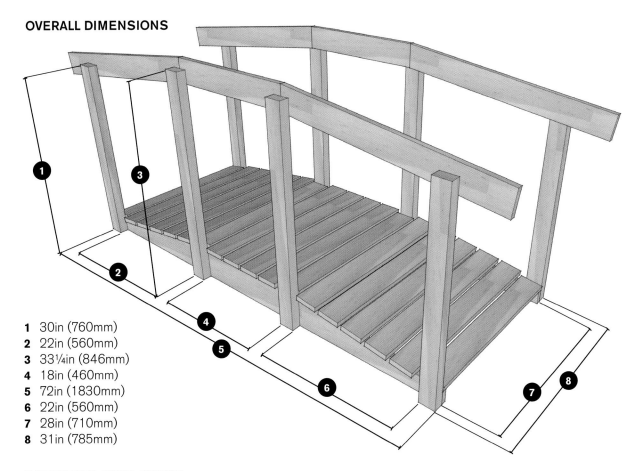

1 30in (760mm)
2 22in (560mm)
3 33¼in (846mm)
4 18in (460mm)
5 72in (1830mm)
6 22in (560mm)
7 28in (710mm)
8 31in (785mm)

MAKING THE BASE

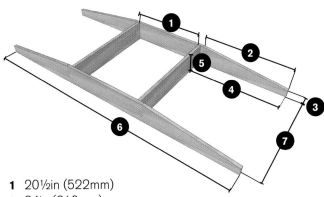

1 20½in (522mm)
2 24in (610mm)
3 2in (50mm)
4 25¼in (641mm)
5 5¼in (135mm)
6 72in (1830mm)
7 26½in (672mm)
All parts made from 1 x 6in (25 x 150mm)

The base of the bridge consists of two tapered sides
and a pair of internal supports. Building the bridge
starts by creating a base. The bridge features ramped
ends, so make a tapered cut on the sides to form
the ramps.

1 Use a square to mark cut lines for cutting parts
to length. The fence of the square should be
tight against the edge of the board before striking
the line. To form the ramped base for the bridge,
cut a pair of 72in (1830mm)-long pieces from 1 x 6in
(25 x 150mm) boards to form the sides. Mark a line
using the square. When you use a saw, the width of
the saw blade creates a narrow kerf where the waste
is removed. For this reason, it's a good idea to mark
an X on the side of the line that will become the waste.
You always cut on the opposite side of the line from
the piece you want to keep.

2 Align the teeth of the saw blade with the line on the waste side and make the cut.

3 With two bridge side pieces cut to 72in (1830mm), lay out the ramps on each end. To do this, mark along the end 2in (50mm) up from what will become the bottom edge. This mark designates one end of the taper for the bridge deck. Do this at both ends of the two bridge sides, taking care to measure from the same edge.

4 Now, measure along the same bottom edge and make a mark at the edge 24in (610mm) from the end.

5 Connect the two marks with a straightedge and draw a line between them. This line forms the taper for the ramped ends of the bridge.

6 To cut these tapers, you can use a circular saw or handsaw. Whichever you use, concentrate on making a straight cut on the waste side of the line. It's easier to start the cut from the end of the board. You'll end up with two boards with a taper at each end. These bridge sides form the foundation for the rest of the bridge structure.

7 Connect the two ramped sides with two pieces 26½in (672mm) long cut from the 1 x 6in (25 x 150mm) boards. Measure 25¼in (640mm) from the end of the bridge side and mark a line using the square to use as a reference aid for assembly. Repeat this for each end of the two bridge sides.

8 Using the reference lines you made on the inside of the bridge sides, line up the two inside support pieces, making sure to position them toward the outside of the line.

9 Use #8 x 2in (4 x 50mm) screws to fasten the internal supports to the bridge sides. Use three screws at each joint.

POSTS

Next, you will be adding the four posts on each side of the base that support the railing. The posts are made from 2x3 (50 x 75mm) stock. You'll need four of them at 30in (760mm) length and four at 33¼in (846mm).

The four posts in the middle of the bridge are longer to allow the handrail to have the same slope as the base. After the posts are cut to length, you will need to fasten them on the outside of the base sides.

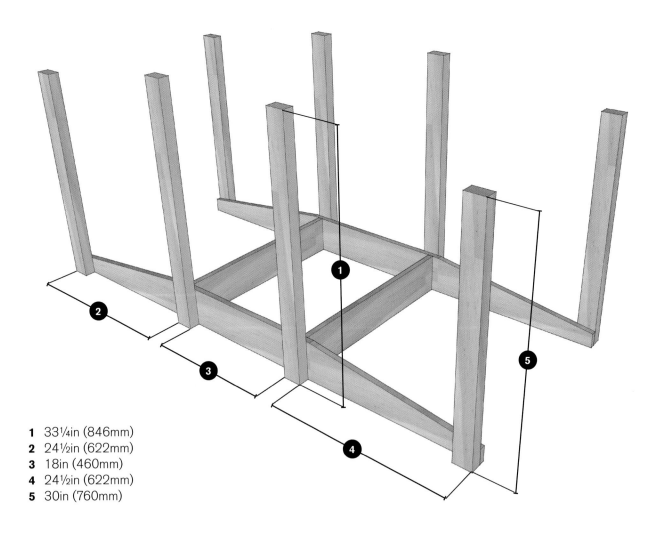

1 33¼in (846mm)
2 24½in (622mm)
3 18in (460mm)
4 24½in (622mm)
5 30in (760mm)

10 Fasten the 30in (760mm) long posts flush with the ends and bottom edge of the sides using #8 x 2in (4 x 50mm) screws driven from the inside of the base. Use three or four screws for these connections. Use a square to aid in alignment when driving the screws. Make sure the fence of the square is tight against the bottom edge of the side.

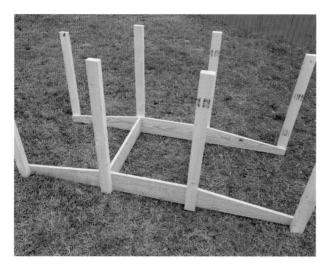

11 To position the longer middle posts, measure 22in (560mm) from the inside edge of the end posts and mark a square line. Use this as an aid to keep the post square to the base as you drive the screws from the inside. These central posts should cover the screws on the bridge base frame.

12 There are 18 floor slats that create the deck of the bridge. Cut the slats from 1 x 4in (25 x 100mm) stock. Cut the four slats between the posts to fit. Cut the remaining to overlap the bridge base by 1in (25mm) on each end. It's a good idea to cut all of the slats and lay them loose in their approximate positions before fixing them in place. Space them by eye for even, appealing spacing.

13 There should be six slats each on the ramped sections and six slats on the flat, center section.

TIP
Before cutting and fastening the slats, check that the base and inner supports are square.

14 Use two screws at each end of the slats to fasten them to the bridge sides. The slats at the ends of the bridge are flush with the ends of the sides, so that's a good place to start fastening them. The two slats at the top of each ramped section should align close to the start of the taper on the base sides. If you find that the wood is splitting, use a countersink bit to predrill the holes then drive the screws just until they're snug. The two slats at the top of each ramped section should align close to the start of the taper on the base sides.

The railing connects the posts on each side and is made from 1 x 4in (25 x 100mm) stock.

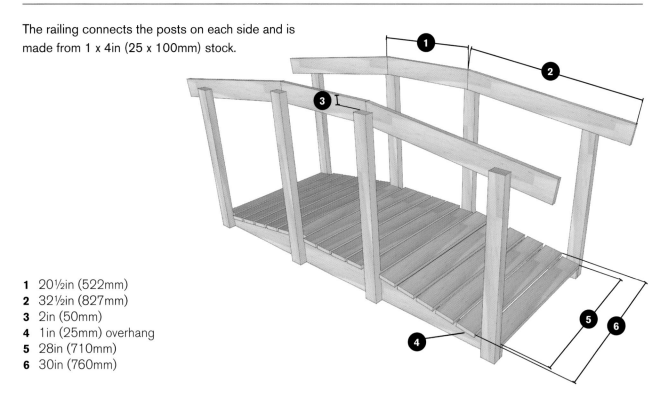

1 20½in (522mm)
2 32½in (827mm)
3 2in (50mm)
4 1in (25mm) overhang
5 28in (710mm)
6 30in (760mm)

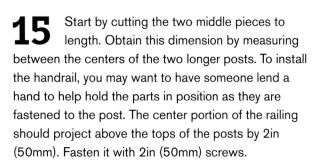

15 Start by cutting the two middle pieces to length. Obtain this dimension by measuring between the centers of the two longer posts. To install the handrail, you may want to have someone lend a hand to help hold the parts in position as they are fastened to the post. The center portion of the railing should project above the tops of the posts by 2in (50mm). Fasten it with 2in (50mm) screws.

16 Adding the remaining pieces of the rail may require some assistance as you mark the angled cuts that join up with the center rail pieces. Start by cutting four pieces of 1 x 4in (25 x 100mm) to 36in (915mm) in length. With the aid of an assistant, hold the piece with one end overlapping the center rail, but with the top corner of each piece aligned. The opposite end should project above the end of the post 2in (50mm). Use a pencil to trace the cut angle against the center rail. Cut this angle using a handsaw then fasten it to the posts. Repeat this process for the other three rail pieces.

17 Mark a line on the end railing piece using the end of the center rail as a guide. This marks the angle to cut the railing for a tight joint.

18 Use a handsaw to make the angled cut on the end of the rail.

19 Fasten the remaining rail pieces to the inside face of the posts, overlapping the end of the post by 2in (50mm). Using 100-grit or 120-grit sandpaper, ease all the rough edges and corners, especially along the top edge of the handrail.

20 Now that the garden bridge is finished, you need only to decide where it will reside in your landscape. To allow air flow under the bridge and to avoid damage from moisture, place concrete pavers or gravel under the bridge to elevate it off the ground, making sure it's level. Make the garden bridge a focal point of your garden or a hidden surprise behind tall plants. It's sure to be a conversation starter. The bridge is ready to become the focal point for your landscape.

Bird-Feeder Stand and Birdhouse

Attracting birds to your backyard is a great way to provide free entertainment. If you love photographing birds, this project also makes it easy for you to get great photos. With plenty of places to hang a variety of feeders and birdhouses, your backyard will become a welcome retreat for a wide variety of bird species. You can build this bird-feeder stand and birdhouse in a matter of hours.

LUMBER REQUIRED

1	3½ x 3½ x 96in (90 x 90 x 2440mm)
4	¾ x 5½ x 96in (19 x 140 x 2440mm)
1	¾ x 2½ x 96in (19 x 63 x 2440mm)
1	1½ x 1½ x 96in (38 x 38 x 2440mm)

MATERIALS REQUIRED

1lb (454g) #8 x 1½in (4 x 40mm) exterior screws

1lb (454g) #8 x 2½in (4 x 60mm) exterior screws

4 screw hooks

OVERALL DIMENSIONS

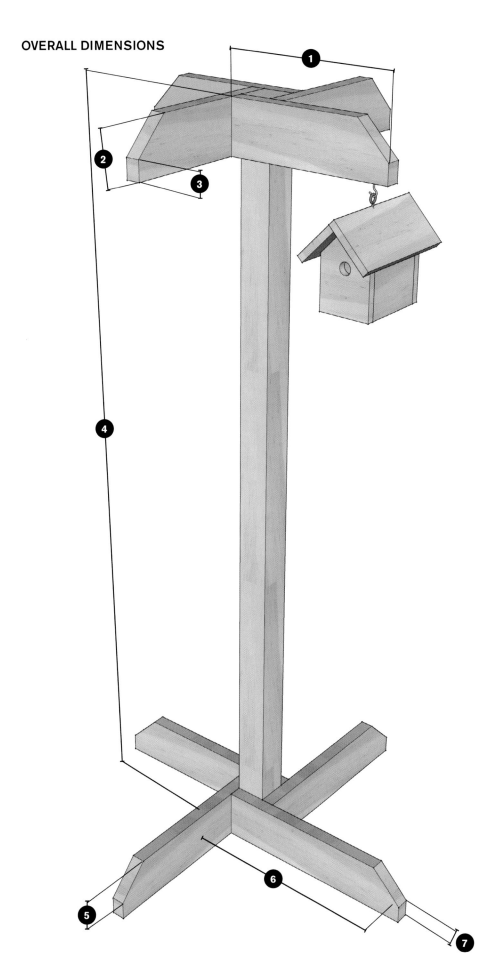

1 18in (455mm)
2 5½in (140mm)
3 2in (50mm)
4 84in (2134mm)
5 5½in (140mm)
6 23¾in (605mm)
7 2in (50mm)

1 To make it easier to reach the top arms for hanging the feeders and houses, cut the post to any length you desire. The post starts out at 96in (2440mm) long, so I cut it down to 84in (2135mm). A handsaw makes quick work of this. After cutting the post to the desired length, the four feet and four arms come next. Cut them from ¾ x 5½in (19 x 140mm) stock. The legs are 23¾in (604mm) long. The arms are 18in (460mm) long.

2 You will now be cutting one corner off each arm and leg at a 45° angle, as shown in the illustration on page 35. This adds a decorative touch and reduces the chance of tripping over the legs. On one end of each arm and leg, make a mark 2in (50mm) from one edge.

3 Use a square to draw a line at 45° from the 2in (50mm) mark.

4 Lopping off the corners or the arms and legs is easy to do with a handsaw or circular saw. If you use a miter saw, set the cut angle to 45°. When cutting the corners of the arms and legs, be sure to cut the corners off the same edge, or the top edge, of each piece.

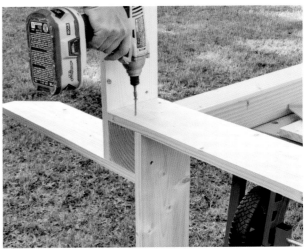

5 With these eight pieces in hand, you can get ready to fasten the legs to the post. Use a square to keep the leg at right angles to the post. The legs should also be flush with the end and the opposite face of the post.

6 Drive one 2½in (60mm) screw to fasten the leg to the post. Make final adjustments for squareness and drive another screw to lock it in place. Work your way around the post to install the remaining legs in the same manner. Repeat the process at the other end to install the arms.

7 The four legs provide a stable base for the bird-feeder stand. To provide more stability for the stand, locate it in a flat, level area. Adding some ground anchors to the legs helps prevent strong winds from toppling the stand. Use screw hooks or screw eyes to hang feeders and houses from the stand. These are common hardware items that are easy to install. Sometimes it helps to drill a small hole before installing the hook.

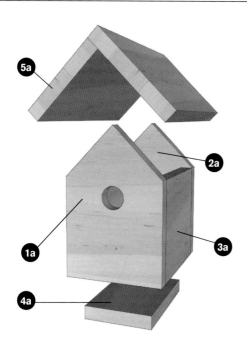

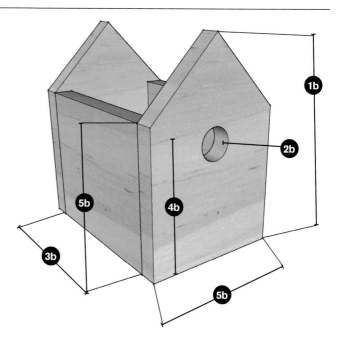

8 The birdhouse is one of those projects that is easy to build in a few hours. Start by cutting the sides, front, back, and pair of roof pieces to length from a ¾ x 5½in (19 x 140mm) board.

1a Front	**1b** 8¼in (210mm)
2a Back	**2b** 1¼in diameter (32mm)
3a Side	**3b** 6½in (165mm)
4a Bottom	**4b** 4½in (115mm)
5a Roof	**5b** 5½in (140mm)

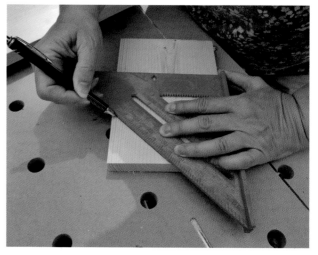

9 After cutting the parts to length, form the peaks for the roof and drill the entry hole for the birds. Lay out the roof lines on the front and back by making a mark at the midpoint of one end.

10 The point of the roof is at the midpoint of the top end of the front and back of the birdhouse. Use the square to locate two lines drawn at 45°, ending at the midpoint you marked earlier. Align the square so that its fence is tight against the edge of the front or back of the birdhouse. Slide the square until the angled edge is aligned with the marked midpoint on the end.

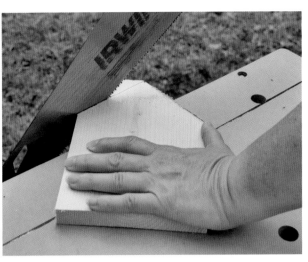

11 Flip the square to the opposite edge and repeat the process, keeping the square tight against the edge.

12 Lop off the corners of the front and back pieces using a handsaw or powered miter saw. Stay tight to the outside of the layout lines.

13 The species of bird you wish to attract determines the size of the entry hole in the front. You can find plenty of charts online to help you make this decision. I used a hole size of 1⅜in (35mm) to attract nuthatches. Use a spade (paddle) bit to drill the entry hole. Use a scrap piece as a backer and securely hold the workpiece when drilling. (NOTE: Drill stopped and hand removed for clarity here.)

14 Now it's time to assemble the birdhouse, starting with the front, back, and then sides. Predrill the holes for the screws and fasten the front and back to the end of the side pieces with 1½in (40mm) screws. Attach the front and back to one of the sides, keeping the pieces flush at the bottom edge. Then flip the assembly over to attach the opposite side.

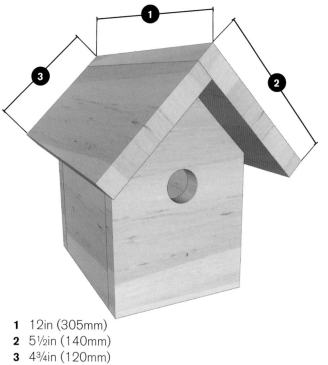

1 12in (305mm)
2 5½in (140mm)
3 4¾in (120mm)

15 Cut the two pieces to length that make up the roof from ¾ x 5½in (19 x 140mm) stock. Because of the way the roof is constructed, you'll also need to remove ¾in (19mm) from the long edge of one of the roof pieces. You can use a handsaw or circular saw to do this. Just make sure to secure the workpiece before sawing.

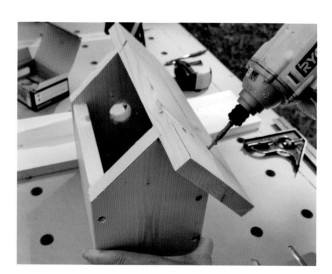

16 Fasten the two roof pieces next, starting with the narrower one of the two. Align one edge with the points on the front and back. The amount of overhang at the front and back is up to you. I centered the roof on my birdhouse front to back. Use 1½in (40mm) screws to fasten the narrow roof piece, aligning the edge at the top of the front and back.

17 Fasten the wider roof piece, keeping it flush with the other roof piece.

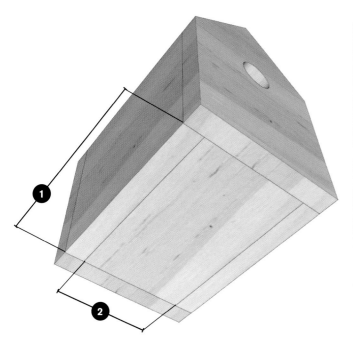

18 The final piece to add is the bottom. Measure the opening at the bottom of the birdhouse and cut a piece to fit loosely.

1 6½in (165mm)
2 4in (100mm)

19 Fasten the bottom in place with four 1½in (40mm) screws, two through each side, as shown. The loose-fitting bottom should provide drainage for any moisture that might enter the birdhouse. To clean out the birdhouse every season, you can flip the bottom down for easier access. Simply remove the two screws toward the front and swing the bottom down, using the rear screws as hinges.

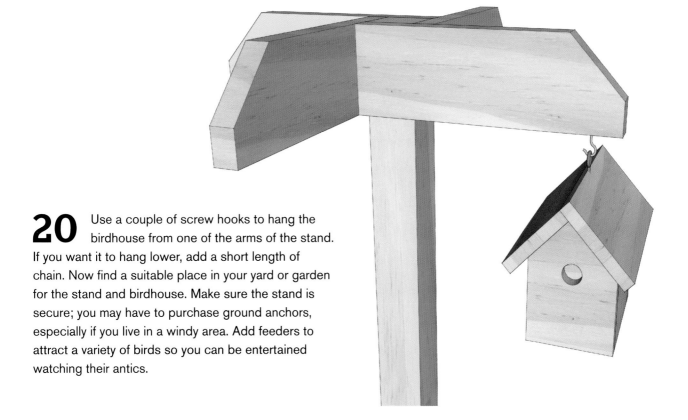

20 Use a couple of screw hooks to hang the birdhouse from one of the arms of the stand. If you want it to hang lower, add a short length of chain. Now find a suitable place in your yard or garden for the stand and birdhouse. Make sure the stand is secure; you may have to purchase ground anchors, especially if you live in a windy area. Add feeders to attract a variety of birds so you can be entertained watching their antics.

Garden Bench

A bench to sit on outdoors provides an inviting spot to relax with a good book, entertain guests, or just enjoy the garden and wildlife. This bench seats two comfortably. While there are a lot of pieces, you'll build subassemblies and then bring them all together to complete the bench.

LUMBER REQUIRED

2 1½ x 3½ x 96in (38 x 90 x 2440mm)
8 ¾ x 3½ x 96in (19 x 90 x 2440mm)
3 ¾ x 2½ x 96in (19 x 63 x 2440mm)

MATERIALS REQUIRED

1lb (454g) #8 x 1¼in (4 x 30mm) exterior screws
1lb (454g) #8 x 2in (4 x 50mm) exterior screws
1lb (454g) #8 x 2½in (4 x 60mm) exterior screws
2 ⁵⁄₁₆ x 3½in (8 x 90mm) carriage bolts with flat washers and hex nuts
2 ⁵⁄₁₆ x 2in (8 x 50mm) carriage bolts with flat washers and hex nuts

OVERALL DIMENSIONS

1 40½in (1027mm)
2 23in (585mm)
3 3½in (90mm)
4 49in (1245mm)

MAKING THE STAND

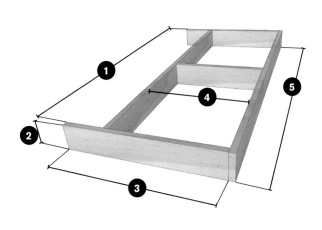

1 The seat frame is the foundation for the bench so that's the best place to start. Cut the two ends, front and back rails, and the center support from ¾ x 3½in (19 x 89mm) boards.

1 44½in (1132mm)
2 3½in (90mm)
3 20¾in (529mm)
4 14½in (367mm)
5 46in (1170mm)

2 Following the dimensions shown, assemble the seat frame with 2in (50mm) screws. Measure and mark the center of the front and back rails to locate the central support. Drive three screws at each connection to create a strong frame. Check that the frame is square as you go.

3 Cutting the legs to length from 1½ x 3½in (38 x 90mm) stock and attaching them to the seat frame is straightforward. But there is something to be aware of: the seat frame is angled to make it more comfortable. Use the dimensions shown on the illustration to locate the legs on the seat frame. It's best to use a flat surface for this process. Start by marking the distance from the bottom of the leg to the seat frame location and draw a line using a square to make a straight line across the leg. When fastening the frame to the legs, the top corner at the back of the seat frame should be flush with the back edge of the rear leg. At the front, the seat frame sits 1¼in (32mm) inside the front edge of the front leg.

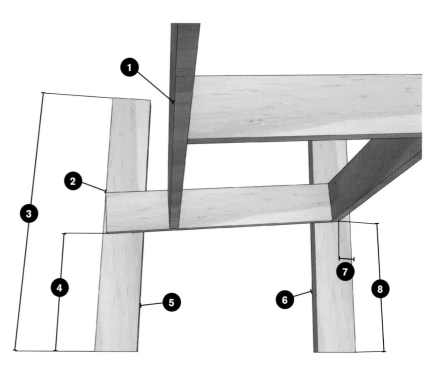

1 Seat frame
2 Back of seat frame flush
   with back of rear leg
3 22¾in (579mm)
4 9⅞in (252mm)
5 Rear leg
6 Front leg
7 1¼in (32mm)
8 11¾in (299mm)

4 The top corner at the back of the seat frame should be flush with the back of the rear leg.

5 The bottom front corner of the seat frame is positioned 11¾in (299mm) up from the bottom of the leg and 1¼in (32mm) in from the front edge of the leg. Check to make sure the legs are parallel with each other and drive one 2in (50mm) screw at each connection. You'll add more screws later after making last-minute adjustments to ensure the bench sits flat on the floor.

6 On a flat surface, attach the seat frame to one pair of legs using 2in (50mm) screws. Use only one screw at each location for now.

7 Use a square to ensure the leg sits flat after the seat frame is attached.

8 If possible, enlist some help to attach the two legs at the opposite end of the seat frame. When all four legs are attached, set the frame and leg assembly on a flat surface and make sure the bottoms of all four legs sit flat. You can also check that the legs are parallel to one another by measuring the distance between them at the top and bottom.

9 Once you're happy with how the assembly sits, drive additional 2in (50mm) screws at each frame and leg connection to create a strong structure.

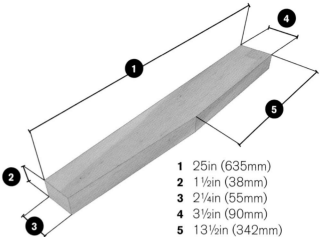

1 25in (635mm)
2 1½in (38mm)
3 2¼in (55mm)
4 3½in (90mm)
5 13½in (342mm)

10 Next, you'll make and attach two arms to the legs and build a frame for the seatback. The seatback connects to the seat frame and arms.

11 The two arms are made from 1½ x 3½in (38 x 90mm) stock. They are tapered from front to back to create a more refined look. A handsaw or circular saw makes quick work of cutting the taper after the arms are cut to length.

TIP
A handsaw or circular saw makes quick work of cutting the taper after the arms are cut to length.

12 After cutting the arms to length, lay out the taper and cut it with a handsaw or circular saw.

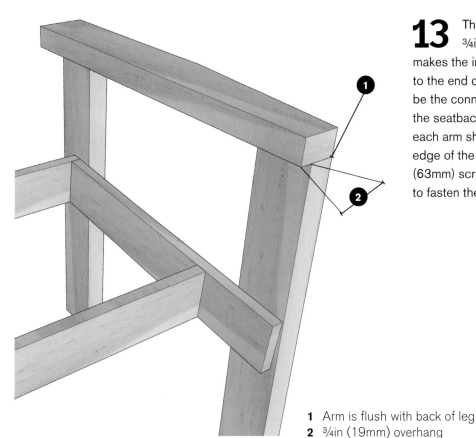

13 The arms overhang the legs ¾in (19mm) on the inside. This makes the inner edge of the arm parallel to the end of the seat frame. These will be the connection points for attaching the seatback frame. The back end of each arm should be even with the back edge of the rear legs. Use two 2½in (63mm) screws at each end of each arm to fasten them to the legs.

1 Arm is flush with back of leg
2 ¾in (19mm) overhang

14 The frame for the seatback is also angled to provide comfort. It is as easy to assemble as the seat frame. It's made from ¾ x 2½in (19 x 63mm) stock. Cut the top and bottom rail, two sides, and center support to length. The sides and center support are the same length. When assembling the seatback frame, bear in mind that the top and bottom rails connect to the ends of the sides and center support, as shown in the illustration.

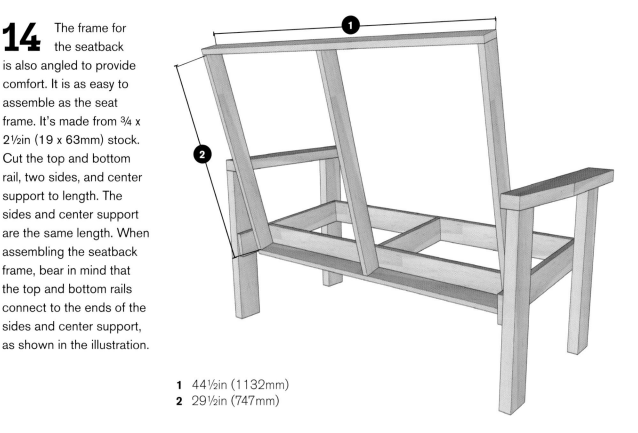

1 44½in (1132mm)
2 29½in (747mm)

15 Assemble the frame with 2in (50mm) screws, with two screws at each connection.

TIP
This is a project that will go a little easier if you have some help but building it yourself is still manageable.

16 There are a few guidelines to keep in mind for properly positioning the frame. You can see the details in the illustration. First, the inside bottom corner of the seatback frame aligns and fits tight to the bottom edge of the back rail on the seat frame. The seatback frame connects to the sides of the seat frame with carriage bolts, but you can use a 1¼in (30mm) screw to temporarily hold the seatback frame in position. The seatback frame is angled and connects to the arms. Again, the final connection will be a carriage bolt through the arm and frame but use a screw for now to hold the frame in place. The back edge of the seatback frame aligns with the top inside corner of the arm.

1 Align seatback frame with back corner of arm
2 Arm
3 Frame flush with back of leg
4 9⅞in (252mm)
5 Edge of seatback frame aligned with bottom edge of seat frame
6 Back leg
7 Front leg
8 23in (585mm)
9 Seat frame
10 Front of seat frame set back 1¼in (30mm) from front of leg
11 11¾in (299mm)
12 1¼in (32mm)

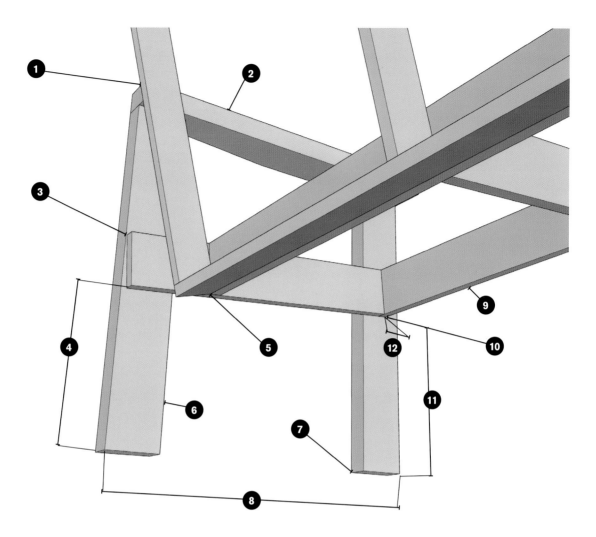

17 Use a screw to temporarily hold the seatback frame in position. Notice that the frame aligns with the upper back corner of the arm.

18 Permanently connect the seatback frame to the arms and seat frame using 5/16in (8mm) carriage bolts, a flat washer, and a hex nut. The bolts make for a super-strong connection. Drill 5/16in (8mm) diameter holes through the arm and seatback frame, using care to center the hole on the joint.

19 Use a hammer to tap a ⁵⁄₁₆ x 3½in (8 x 90mm) carriage bolt through the arm and frame.

20 Place a flat washer and hex nut on the carriage bolt and tighten the nut securely.

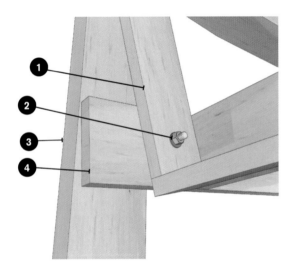

21 Connect the bottom of the seatback frame to the seat frame in a similar fashion. Drill a hole through the sides of both frames and connect them with a ⁵⁄₁₆ x 2in (8 x 50mm) carriage bolt, washer, and nut as before.

1 Seatback frame
2 ⁵⁄₁₆ x 2in (8 x 50mm) carriage bolt with washer and nut
3 Rear leg
4 Seat frame

22 The slats on the seat and seatback complete the assembly. There are five slats each on the seat and seatback. It's easy to set up an assembly line process to cut them all to length from ¾ x 3½in (19 x 90mm) stock. Attach the slats on the seat first. Fasten the slats with 2in (50mm) screws, two at each end (see Tip on facing page). The front slat on the seat should overhang the seat frame and align with the front edge of the front legs. Space the remaining slats visually and fasten them in place. Position the rear slat tight against the seatback frame.

23 Add the final slats to the seatback. Here, the slats are spaced farther apart. The top slat should align and sit flush with the top of the seatback frame. The bottom slat is spaced ¾in (19mm) above the seat slats. To create this spacing, I used a couple of ¾in (19mm)-thick cutoffs to act as spacers for the bottom slat. This spacing helps drain water during rains and prevents debris from building up on the seat.

24 When attaching the first few slats to the seatback, ensure the frame is square before driving the screws. With the top and bottom slats fastened in place, the remaining three slats should be equally spaced. Here again, a pair of spacers come to the rescue to ensure accurate spacing. I used cutoffs cut to 2¼in (55mm) length. Work your way from the bottom up by positioning a spacer at each end of the previous slat and setting the next slat on top of the spacers before driving the screws.

25 The assembly is complete but there's one other thing you should do before putting the bench to use. Use 100-grit sandpaper to sand all surfaces smooth and ease the sharp edges to make sitting on the bench more comfortable. All you need to do now is decide where to place the bench in your landscape. Should you place it in a secluded corner or prominently display it as an inviting retreat for family members and guests? The decision is yours.

Wall Sconce

Having an outdoor light in your landscape or near your porch or deck not only sets the mood, it can also contribute to safety at night. This simple wall sconce is an easy build using only three pieces of wood and some molding from the lumber store. It can be mounted almost anywhere, including a post or fence rail, and uses a pair of exterior-rated, battery-operated LED lights. The lights I used include a remote that allows you to switch the lights on and off. The remote also controls the color of the lights, so you can set the mood simply by selecting the color of your choice.

LUMBER REQUIRED

1 ¾ x 5½ x 24in (19 x 140 x 610mm)

8 ¾ x 3½ x 24in (19 x 90 x 610mm)

1 ⅜ x 1¼ x 84in (10 x 32 x 2135mm) door-stop molding

MATERIALS REQUIRED

1lb (454kg) box #8 x 2in (4 x 50mm) exterior screws

1lb (454kg) box #8 x 1¼in (4 x 30mm) exterior screws

1lb (454kg) box #8 x 1in (4 x 25mm) round-head or pan-head stainless steel wood screws

2 Exterior-rated battery-operated LED lights (Lumabase 69102 battery-operated LED submersible lights)

Exterior-rated double-sided tape or mounting squares

Exterior-grade paint

OVERALL DIMENSIONS

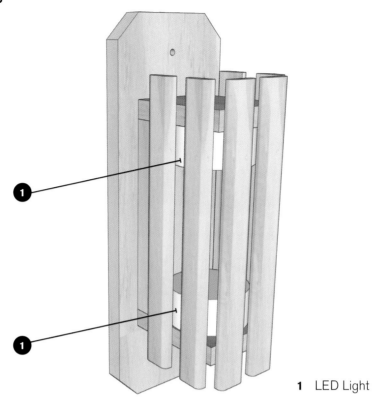

1 LED Light

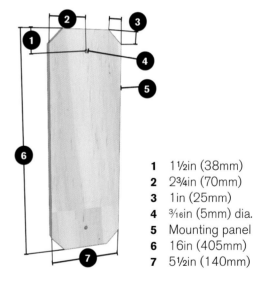

1 1½in (38mm)
2 2¾in (70mm)
3 1in (25mm)
4 ³⁄₁₆in (5mm) dia.
5 Mounting panel
6 16in (405mm)
7 5½in (140mm)

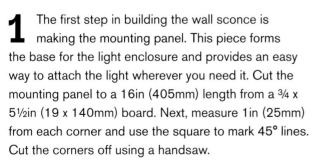

1 The first step in building the wall sconce is making the mounting panel. This piece forms the base for the light enclosure and provides an easy way to attach the light wherever you need it. Cut the mounting panel to a 16in (405mm) length from a ¾ x 5½in (19 x 140mm) board. Next, measure 1in (25mm) from each corner and use the square to mark 45° lines. Cut the corners off using a handsaw.

2 Drill two ³⁄₁₆in (5mm) diameter mounting holes in the mounting panel at the locations shown in the illustration.

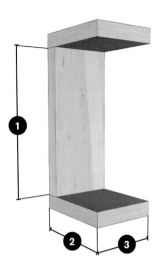

3 Set the mounting plate aside for now so you can concentrate on making the enclosure for the LED lights. It starts with three pieces cut from ¾ x 3½in (19 x 90mm) stock—a top, bottom, and back.

1 8in (200mm)
2 4½in (115mm)
3 3½in (90mm)

4 You'll be using exterior-rated double-sided tape to fasten the LED lights to the inside top and bottom of the enclosure. To provide a smooth surface for the tape adhesive, apply a few coats of an exterior-grade paint, allowing each coat to dry before applying the next coat. Apply masking tape to the edges to maintain a clean paint line.

5 To assemble the enclosure, fasten the top and bottom to the end of the back using 2in (50mm) screws.

6 Before mounting the enclosure structure to the mounting plate, fasten the LED lights using double-sided mounting tape rated for exterior use. Make sure the tape is secure to the top and bottom of the enclosure and tight to the back of the LED light. In some cases, the double-sided tape may not be appropriate, especially if the back of the light is not flat. You may have to remove the cover of the light, drill a couple of holes and fasten the back to the enclosure, then reattach the light's cover.

7 Set the light in place and apply firm pressure to secure it.

8 Center the enclosure on the mounting plate and fasten it from the back side using four 1¼in (30mm) screws.

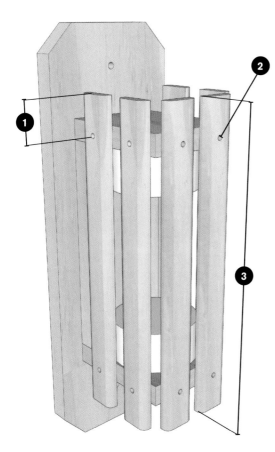

1   1⅜in (35mm)
2   ³⁄₁₆in (5mm)-dia. hole
3   11½in (292mm)

9 The last step is to add the vertical slats that make up the outside of the enclosure. They are made from standard ⅜in-thick x 1¼in-wide (10 x 32mm) door-stop molding. Cut six pieces 11½in (292mm) long. Align the slats on the work surface and use a square to mark hole locations for the screws you'll use to fasten the slats to the bracket. The holes are located 1⅜in (35mm) from each end.

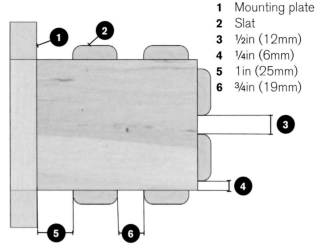

1 Mounting plate
2 Slat
3 ½in (12mm)
4 ¼in (6mm)
5 1in (25mm)
6 ¾in (19mm)

10 Place some scrap pieces of wood under the slats to prepare for drilling the ³⁄₁₆in (5mm)-diameter clearance holes for the screws. The scrap pieces help protect the work surface when drilling through the slats.

11 With the LED lights in place and operational, you can fasten the slats to the bracket. The slats extend 1in (25mm) above and below the bracket. The illustration shows a top view with dimensions for locating the slats.

12 Position the slat and use a ¹⁄₁₆in (1.5mm) drill bit to drill a pilot hole for the screw, using the hole in the slat as a guide for positioning the drill bit. Drilling pilot holes for the screws makes it easier to tighten them down.

13 Using #8 x 1in (4 x 25mm) round-head or pan-head wood screws, fasten each slat in place. Be sure to keep the ends of the slats aligned with one another. Now you need to decide where you're going to hang the light. Just be sure to use appropriate fasteners that are strong enough to support the weight and are suitable for the surface where the wall sconce is attached. Setting the mood in your landscape is as easy as pressing a couple of buttons on the remote.

Planter Box

If you enjoy growing flowers or vegetables, you'll appreciate this planter box. Easy and quick to build, it consists of two simple frames joined by four legs. The planter box uses a heavy-duty storage bin to contain the soil. The width and length of the box are dictated by the size of bin, so you'll need to have the bin on hand before you start building the planter. I chose a 10-gallon (45 liter) bin.

A great feature of the planter box is its adjustability. The vertical placement of the lower shelf is determined by the height of the plastic bin and whether you want it recessed or flush with the top of the planter.

LUMBER REQUIRED

1   1½ x 2½ x 96in (38 x 63 x 2440mm)
8   ¾ x 2½ x 96in (19 x 63 x 2440mm)

MATERIALS REQUIRED

1lb (454g) #8 x 1¼ (4 x 30mm) exterior screws
1lb (454g) #8 x 2in (4 x 50mm) exterior screws
1   heavy-duty plastic bin

OVERALL DIMENSIONS

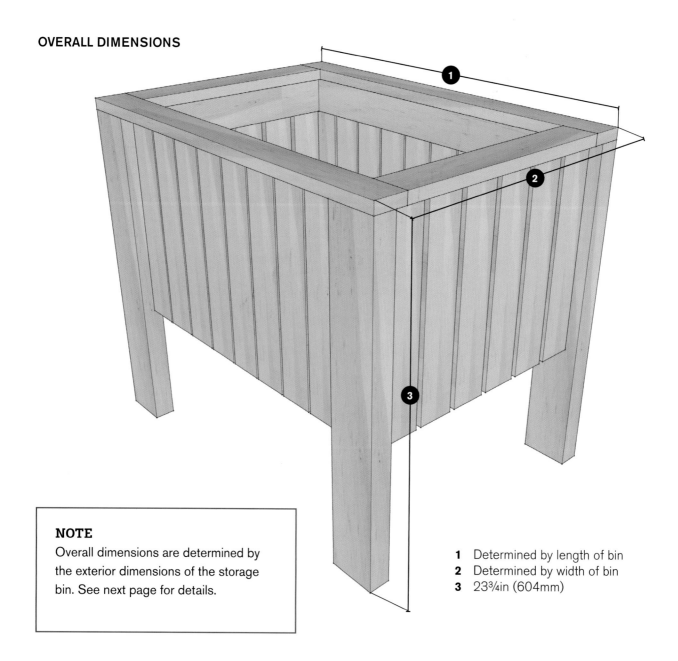

NOTE
Overall dimensions are determined by the exterior dimensions of the storage bin. See next page for details.

1   Determined by length of bin
2   Determined by width of bin
3   23¾in (604mm)

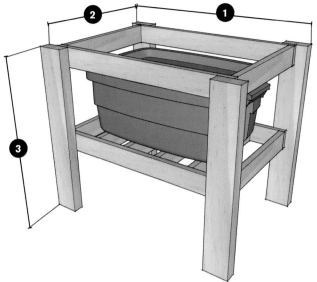

1 A heavy-duty plastic bin creates the container for soil and plants in the planter box. The first order of business is to measure the maximum outside width and length of the storage bin you wish to use, without the lid. Make sure to include the handles in the length measurement. These dimensions become the inside dimensions of the two finished frames for the planter box. The frames must fit around the bin.

2 Using the dimensions of the bin, cut the pieces that make up the top and bottom frames from ¾ x 2½in (19 x 63mm) boards. Keep in mind that the fronts and backs of the frames should be 1½in (38mm) longer than the overall outside length of the plastic bin. The length of the end pieces (and internal pieces of the bottom frame) should equal the width of the bin.

1 Determined by length of bin
2 Determined by width of bin
3 23in (585mm)

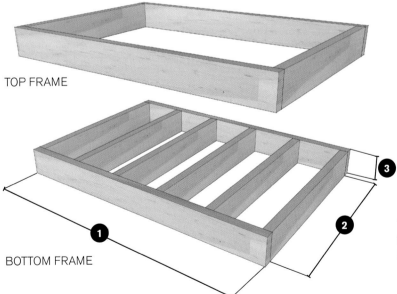

TOP FRAME

BOTTOM FRAME

1 Determined by length of bin
2 Determined by width of bin
3 2½in (63mm)

3 Assemble the two frames with the shorter end pieces between the longer front and back pieces.

4 Fasten the frame pieces using 2in (50mm) screws at each corner.

5 Select one of the frames that will serve as the lower frame and support for the plastic bin. Attach the four additional internal supports, spacing them equally. These supports create a solid foundation for the plastic bin when it is loaded with soil and plants.

6 The four legs connect the two frames that make up the "bones" of the planter box. Cut the legs to length from a 1½ x 2½in (38 x 63mm) board.

7 Now is a good time to determine the vertical position of the lower frame. I positioned the lower frame so that the upper edge of the plastic bin would be at a height equal to the bottom edge of the top frame. Mark the position on the inside of each leg.

1 25½in (647mm)
2 Determined by
   depth of bin
3 2½in (63mm)

8 Inset the frames 1½in (38mm) from the outside edge of the legs.

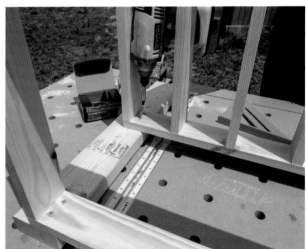

9 Check to make sure the frames are square to the legs before fastening them with 2in (50mm) screws.

10 The skeleton of the planter box is now ready for the slats to be added for the finishing touch.

11 If you wish, you can now get creative and use slats of varying widths. I chose to make all the slats from the same ¾ x 2½in (19 x 63mm) material used for the frames. The number and spacing of slats on the four sides will vary depending on the final size of leg and frame assembly.

1 Slat length

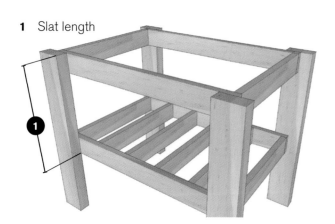

12 Cut the slats to a length equal to or greater than the distance between the top of the upper frame and the bottom of the lower frame. Arrange them on each side of the planter box.

13 Once the slats are arranged, fasten them to the upper and lower frames at each end with 1¼in (30mm) screws.

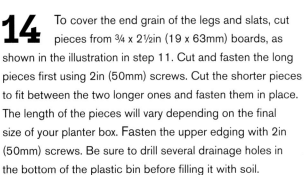

14 To cover the end grain of the legs and slats, cut pieces from ¾ x 2½in (19 x 63mm) boards, as shown in the illustration in step 11. Cut and fasten the long pieces first using 2in (50mm) screws. Cut the shorter pieces to fit between the two longer ones and fasten them in place. The length of the pieces will vary depending on the final size of your planter box. Fasten the upper edging with 2in (50mm) screws. Be sure to drill several drainage holes in the bottom of the plastic bin before filling it with soil.

15 Your planter box is complete and ready for your selection of decorative plants. All that's left to do now is decide where you want to place it.

Wishing Well

Nothing attracts attention to your garden landscape more than an old-fashioned wishing well. This one includes a working crank to raise and lower a pail. Fill the base and pail with greenery and flowers, then watch your friends and family give the hand crank a try.

LUMBER REQUIRED

1	1½ x 2½ x 96in (38 x 63 x 2440mm)
3	1½ x 3½ x 96in (38 x 90 x 2440mm)
1	¾ x 2½ x 96in (19 x 63 x 2440mm)
5	¾ x 3½ x 96in (19 x 90 x 2440mm)
1	¾-dia. x 48in (19 x 1220mm) dowel

MATERIALS REQUIRED

	1lb (454g) #8 x 1½in (4 x 40mm) exterior screws
	1lb (454g) #8 x 2in (4 x 50mm) exterior screws
	1lb (454g) #8 x 3in (4 x 80mm) exterior screws
	1 ⅜ x 72in (9.5 x 1830mm) twisted sisal rope
1	5qt (4l) galvanized bucket

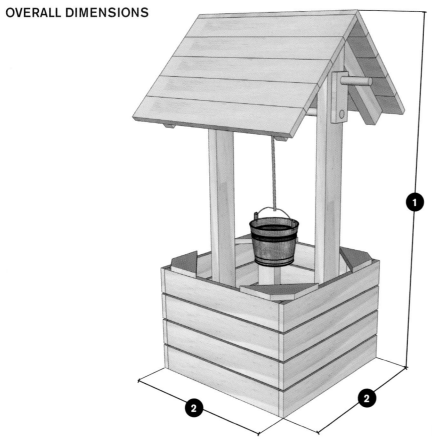

1 48in (1220mm)
2 22in (560mm)

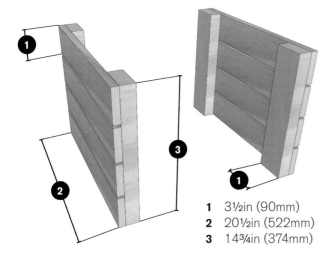

1 3½in (90mm)
2 20½in (522mm)
3 14¾in (374mm)

1 The base of the wishing well consists of four corner posts connected by slats. You'll be making two assemblies that make up the front and back of the base. Cut the slats and posts to length from ¾ x 3½in (19 x 90mm) and 1½ x 3½in (38 x 90mm) boards respectively.

2 Use 1½in (40mm) screws to fasten the slats to the posts. Fasten the top and bottom slats first, keeping them flush with the ends of the posts. Use a square to help align these slats.

1 22in (560mm)

3 Complete the front and back assemblies by fastening the remaining slats, spacing them evenly.

4 You now need to connect the front and back panels with the side slats. Cut the side slats to length from ¾ x 3½in (19 x 90mm) boards.

5 Use a square to help align the side slats while fastening them to the posts with 1½in (40mm) screws.

6 Complete the base with the remaining slats to create a box.

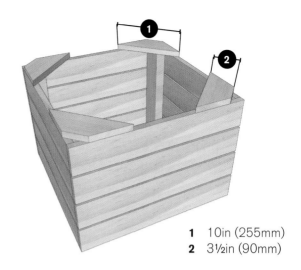

1 10in (255mm)
2 3½in (90mm)

7 Fasten the braces at each corner using 1½in (40mm) screws.

8 To help keep the base square and stable, cut corner braces that fit on top of the base from ¾ x 3½in (19 x 90mm) boards.

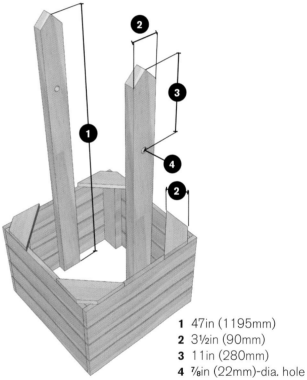

1 47in (1195mm)
2 3½in (90mm)
3 11in (280mm)
4 ⅞in (22mm)-dia. hole

9 Fasten the braces at each corner using 1½in (40mm) screws.

10 The vertical posts support the roof and crank mechanism for raising and lowering the pail; they are cut from 1½ x 3½in (38 x 90mm) stock.

11 Mark the midpoint at the end of the post then use a square to mark lines at 45° that meet at the midpoint. Remove the waste with a saw. After cutting the corners off one end of each post, you can drill the holes for the crank rod now or wait until later.

12 Center the post on the width of the base's side. Use a square to ensure the posts remain vertical as you drive the screws.

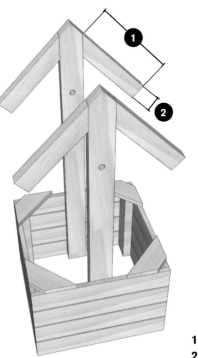

1 13¾in (349mm)
2 2½in (63mm)

13 With the post vertical, fasten the posts to the sides of the base with 2in (50mm) screws from the outside.

14 Next, you'll add the "rafters" that support the roof. They're lengths of 1½ x 2½in (38 x 63mm) with a 45° cut at one end.

15 Fasten the rafters in place with a pair of 3in (80mm) screws driven horizontally into the posts, aligning the top edge with the mitered cut on the post.

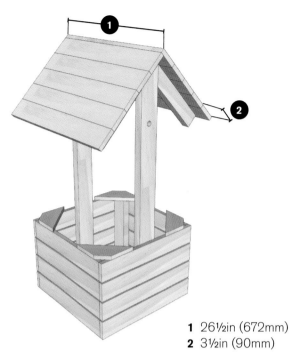

1 26½in (672mm)
2 3½in (90mm)

16 Give the wishing well a roof by cutting planks to length from ¾ x 3½in (19 x 90mm) boards.

17 Fasten the roof planks in place using 1½in (40mm) screws.

TIP

A slightly oversized hole allows the dowel for the crank mechanism to spin freely.

18 Next comes the fun part of adding the crank mechanism for raising and lowering the pail. It's made from a length of ¾in (19mm) dowel, a crank block, and handle and an end block. If you haven't already, drill a ⅞in (22mm)-dia. hole in each post 11in (280mm) from the top of the post. To create a clean hole with little splintering, drill from one side just until the tip breaks through the opposite side of the workpiece. Then complete the hole from the opposite side, using the small hole to center and guide the bit.

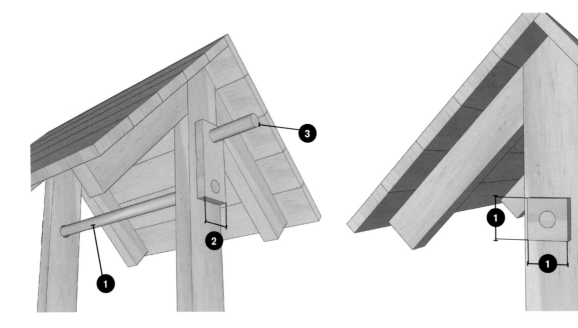

1 1in (25mm) dowel x 22⅜in (570mm) long
2 2½in (63mm)
3 1in (25mm) dowel x 4¾in (120mm) long

1 2½in (63mm)

19 Now you can build the crank mechanism. Start by cutting a ¾in (19mm)-dia. dowel to length for the main shaft. You'll want to make sure the dowel is long enough to accommodate the crank and end block plus about ⅛in (3mm) to allow the shaft to spin freely. In short, measure the outside-to-outside distance of the posts at the hole location and add 1⅝in (40mm) to obtain the final length of the dowel. While you're at it, cut the short piece of dowel that forms the handle of the crank. To hold the longer dowel in place, cut a crank block and end block from ¾ x 2½in (19 x 63mm) stock. Carefully drill the ¾in (19mm)-dia. holes

in each piece. To attach each of the blocks to the main shaft and handle, predrill a clearance hole for a screw through the side of the block, centered on the center of the hole. The hole size should be just large enough to allow the threads of the screw to pass through easily. Place the blocks on the ends of the shaft and insert the handle. Use the holes in the blocks as a guide to drill a ³⁄₃₂in (2mm) pilot hole just through the dowel. This helps the screw go in more easily without the risk of splitting the dowel. Drive a screw through the predrilled hole, just snugging it up. Tightening the screw too much may split the wood.

20 To secure the handle to the crank block and the blocks at each end of the main shaft, use a 1½in (40mm) screw, tightening it just until it's snug against the block. All that's left to do now is tie one end of a few feet of sisal rope to the shaft and use the crank to wind a few feet around the shaft. Tie the opposite end of the rope around a small pail to create a fun and "functional" wishing well. It's sure to attract a lot of attention in your landscape.

Pergola

Providing a welcoming entryway into your garden, this pergola invites people to explore. It's a simple structure consisting of four posts with lattice sides and a simple slat roof that encourages climbing vines to grow. It's an easy build, but you'll need some help with the assembly.

LUMBER REQUIRED

4   3½ x 3½ x 96in (90 x 90 x 2440mm)
15   ¾ x 1½ x 72in (19 x 38 x 1830mm)
2   ¾ x 5½ x 72in (19 x 140 x 1830mm)
4   ¾ x 2½ x 96in (19 x 63 x 2440mm)

MATERIALS REQUIRED

1lb (454g) #8 x 1¼in (4 x 30mm) exterior screws
1lb (454g) #8 x 1½in (4 x 40mm) exterior screws
1lb (454g) #8 x 2in (4 x 50mm) exterior screws
8   5⁄16 x 5in (8 x 130mm) carriage bolts with flat washers and hex nuts
Exterior wood glue

NOTES ON CONSTRUCTION

Building a standing structure sometimes requires a permit from your local building department, especially if the posts are permanently anchored into the ground. Check with the officials in your area before starting. Another consideration is how it will be anchored to the ground. Left freestanding, it could be blown over by a strong wind. You could purchase posts longer than 96in (2440mm) and bur them in the ground. You could also use steel post anchors like the ones shown on page 73 – one type feature a long spike that you drive into the ground with a mallet; the other bolts to a flat surface. Again, be sure to check with local building officials for guidance.

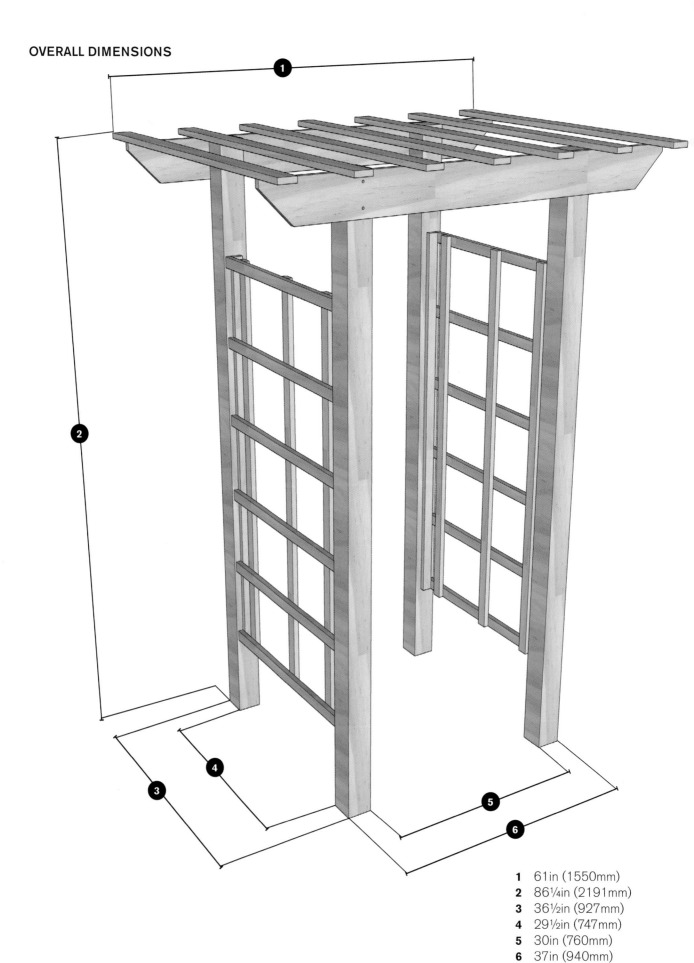

1   61in (1550mm)
2   86¼in (2191mm)
3   36½in (927mm)
4   29½in (747mm)
5   30in (760mm)
6   37in (940mm)

You drive this post anchor into the ground and then fasten the post to it.

This post anchor can be mounted on a deck or patio. Just make sure to use the appropriate anchors or fasteners.

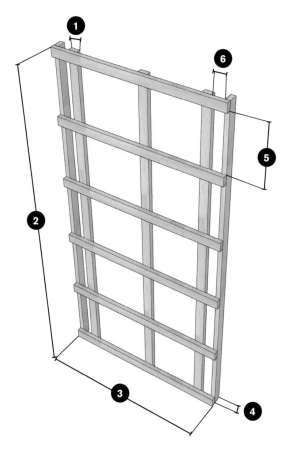

1 Start by cutting the parts for the lattice panels from ¾ x 1½in (19 x 38mm) boards.

2 Before fastening each piece in place, make sure it's square to the adjoining piece. Mark its position and predrill a small pilot hole (³⁄₃₂in/2mm) for the screw through the top piece and just into the bottom piece. Do this at each intersection. Then remove the top piece and apply exterior wood glue. The addition of exterior wood glue at every joint creates a strong panel.

1 1½in (38mm)
2 58in (1475mm)
3 29½in (747mm)
4 1½in (38mm)
5 9¾in (250mm)
6 2in (50mm)

3 Now drive a 1¼in (32mm) screw at each intersection, checking again to make sure the assembly is square as you go.

4 The completed panels connect to the front and back posts to form the two sides of the pergola. Cut the posts from the 3½ x 3½ (90 x 90mm) stock.

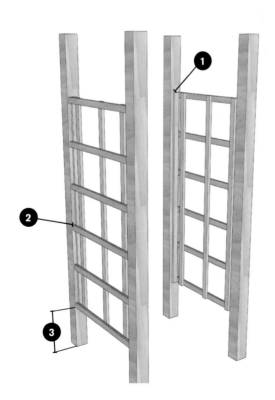

5 Attach each panel to the front and back post. Locate the lattice panel 12in (305mm) from the bottom of the post and set back ¼in (6mm) from the outside face of the post before fastening it with 2in (50mm) screws through the side rails of the panels on the inside.

1 Fasten panel to post through side of panel
2 Panel set back ¼in (6mm) from face of posts
3 12in (305mm)

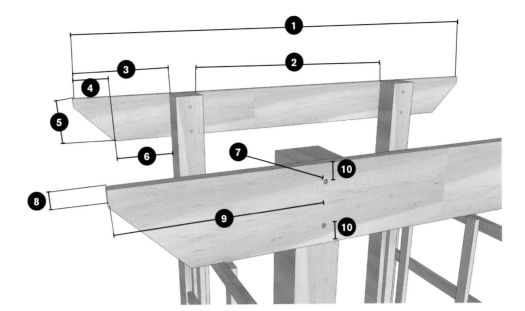

1 61in (1550mm)
2 30in (760mm)
3 12in (305mm)
4 4½in (115mm)
5 5½in (140mm)
6 7½in (190mm)
7 ⁵⁄₁₆in (8mm)-dia.
8 1in (25mm)
9 13¾in (349mm)
10 1¼in (32mm)

6 The "roof" structure comes next. For this, you're going to want to call in some assistance. You'll need some help to hold the side assemblies in place as you fasten the two beams that connect the sides of the pergola.

NOTE

You have the option here of anchoring the side assemblies in the ground then adding the roof structure. Otherwise, you can complete the structure and then set it in place with some help from a few friends. If you choose the latter option, add a temporary brace at the bottom front and back to keep the posts square to the roof assembly as you move the structure into position. The side-to-side distance between the posts should be equal.

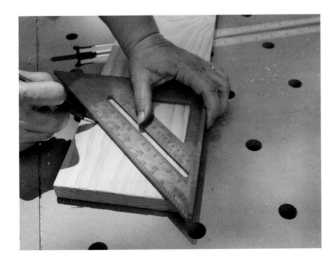

7 Make the beams from ¾ x 5½in (19 x 140mm) boards. Cut the beams to length. Make a mark 1in (25mm) from the top edge of the beam then use the speed square to draw a line from the mark to the bottom edge.

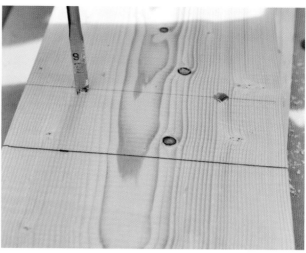

8 Use the square to guide the saw for a clean, straight cut.

9 The beams project 12in (305mm) beyond the posts, so measure and mark a guideline from each end. Drill $5/16$in (8mm) holes for the carriage bolts that secure the beams to the posts.

10 With some assistance, locate the beams on the posts, ensuring they are square to the posts. Use the holes in the beam to mark the holes in the posts. Remove the beam, then drill through the post.

11 Fasten the beams in place with carriage bolts, washers, and nuts.

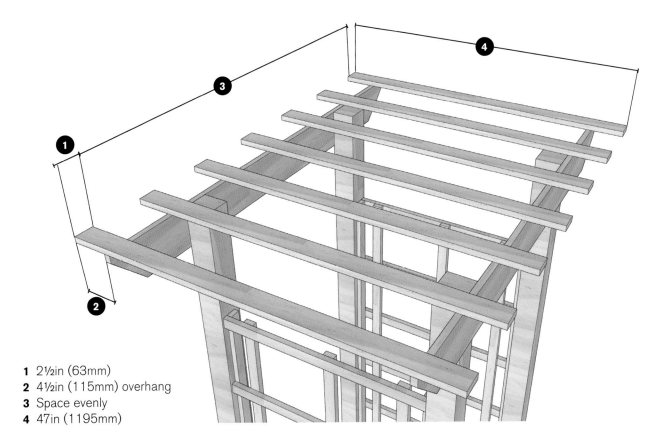

1 2½in (63mm)
2 4½in (115mm) overhang
3 Space evenly
4 47in (1195mm)

12 To complete the structure, make the slats that connect the front and rear beams. Cut these from ¾ x 2½in (19 x 63mm) boards.

13 Fasten the slats to the beams with 1½in (40mm) screws. If you have opted to complete the pergola in preparation for setting it in place, use long strips of wood fastened at the front and back at the bottom of the posts. Just make sure the assembly is still square by checking that the distance between the side posts is the same at the top and bottom. Depending on how you anchor the pergola to the ground, ensure the roof structure is level and the posts are plumb (not leaning in any direction). Perhaps you can head to the garden nursery and pick out some fragrant, beautiful flowers and vines to surround the new addition to your landscape.

Barbecue Workstation

This workstation becomes a handy addition to your outdoor grill to hold meats, condiments, and grilling accessories. Some hooks on the back wall will be useful for hanging grilling utensils while the top shelf is great to keep grilling seasonings to hand. This unit is also at home in the garden shed as a potting station for planting and repotting plants, complete with hooks for hanging gardening tools and a shelf for storing gardening chemicals. The construction of the workstation is simple. Two frames form the foundation for the worktop and bottom shelf. These frames are joined by the four legs, with the rear legs extending up to form a backstop and narrow shelf.

LUMBER REQUIRED

9   ¾ x 3½ x 96in (19 x 90 x 2440mm)
4   1½ x 3½ x 96in (38 x 90 x 2440mm)

MATERIALS REQUIRED

1lb (454g) #8 x 1½in (4 x 40mm) exterior screws
1lb (454g) #8 x 2in (4 x 50mm) exterior screws

OVERALL DIMENSIONS

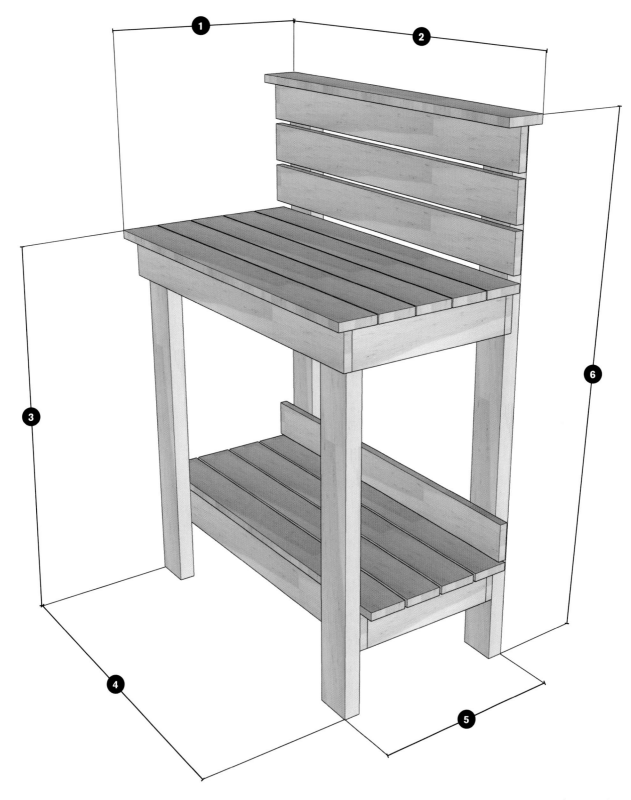

1 19½in (497mm)
2 35½in (902mm)
3 34¾in (884mm)
4 32½in (827mm)
5 17¾in (449mm)
6 47¾in (1214mm)

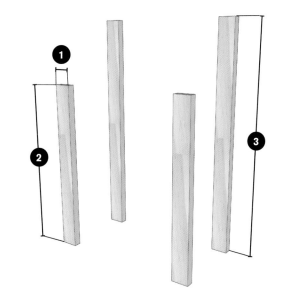

1. 3½in (90mm)
2. 34in (865mm)
3. 47in (1195mm)
4. 34in (865mm)
5. 15½in (392mm)
6. 3½in (90mm)
7. Top frame
8. 32½in (827mm)
9. 13¼in (336mm)
10. 3½in (90mm)
11. Bottom frame

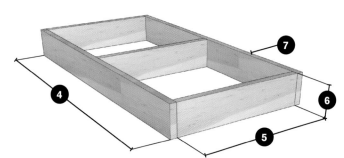

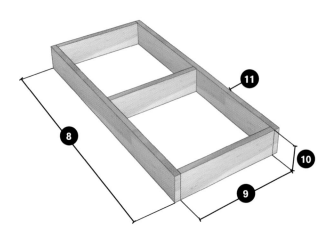

1 Start by cutting the four legs to length from 1½ x 3½in (38 x 90mm) stock. Set the legs aside as you work on building the upper and lower frames from ¾ x 3½in (19 x 90mm) boards.

2 Join the front and back rails of each frame with two ends and a central support. Fasten the joints with 2in (50mm) screws, checking that all the joints of the frames are square first.

3 Next you will be fastening the frames to the legs.

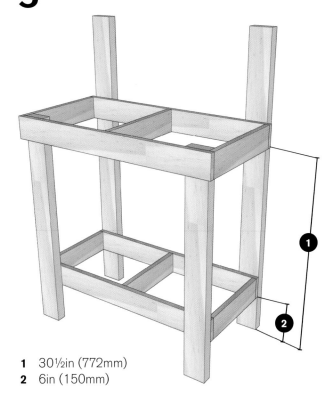

1 30½in (772mm)
2 6in (150mm)

4 To locate the lower frame, use the square as a guide to mark a line 6in (150mm) from the bottom of each leg on the inside face.

5 Use the square to position the frame on the legs before fastening the frame to each leg using 2in (50mm) screws.

6 Position the upper frame flush with the top of the front legs and 30½in (772mm) from the bottom of the rear legs. Fasten using 2in (50mm) screws.

7 Next cut the slats to length from ¾ x 3½in (19 x 90mm) boards. Fortunately, they are all the same length.

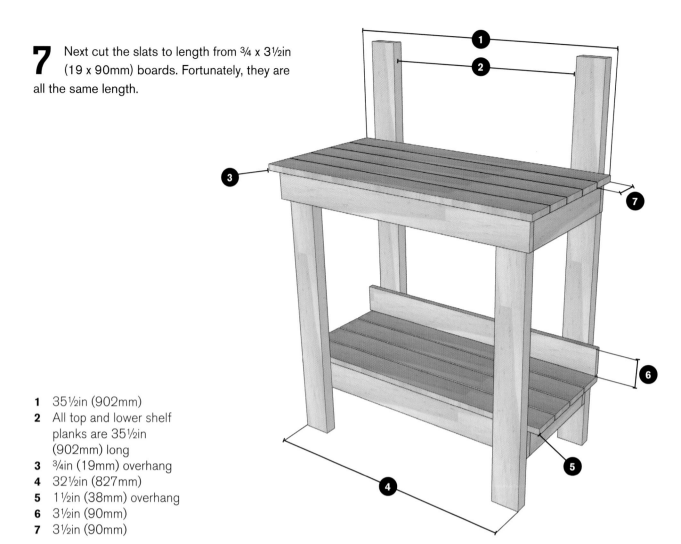

1 35½in (902mm)
2 All top and lower shelf planks are 35½in (902mm) long
3 ¾in (19mm) overhang
4 32½in (827mm)
5 1½in (38mm) overhang
6 3½in (90mm)
7 3½in (90mm)

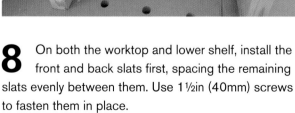

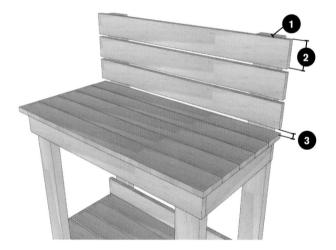

8 On both the worktop and lower shelf, install the front and back slats first, spacing the remaining slats evenly between them. Use 1½in (40mm) screws to fasten them in place.

1 Upper plank flush with top of rear leg
2 3½in (90mm)
3 ¾in (19mm)

9 When fastening the slats that form the back wall of the workstation, locate them ¾in (19mm) above the horizontal surface using scrap stock as a spacer. Fasten the bottom and top slats before fastening the remainder.

10 Make sure the top slat is flush with the top of the rear legs.

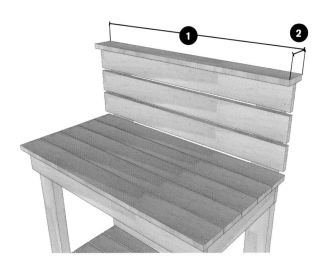

1   35½in (902mm)
2   3½in (90mm)

11 Install the shelf flush with the back of the rear legs using 2in (50mm) screws. Once you locate the workstation where you wish and start using it, you'll quickly discover how practical and handy it is then wonder how you ever got along without it.

Deck Tray

When entertaining guests in a garden or on a backyard deck, there's often a shortage of surfaces, especially when food has been served and everyone is looking for a place to enjoy their snacks. If you have a fence or a deck with a railing along the perimeter, this deck tray solves the problem. It fits snugly over the top of the deck rail and provides a flat, stable surface for food and drink. It's also handy to have on hand near the grill for holding condiments and other grilling items. Make a few to have on hand for your next get-together. The construction of the deck tray couldn't be easier. Four boards make up the base of the tray, a lip along three edges on top holds everything together, and two cleats on the bottom fit over your deck rail.

LUMBER REQUIRED

3	¾ x 3½ x 96in (19 x 90 x 2440mm)
1	¾ x 1½ x 72in (19 x 38 x 1830mm)

MATERIALS REQUIRED

1lb (454g) #8 x 1½in (4 x 40mm) exterior screws

OVERALL DIMENSIONS

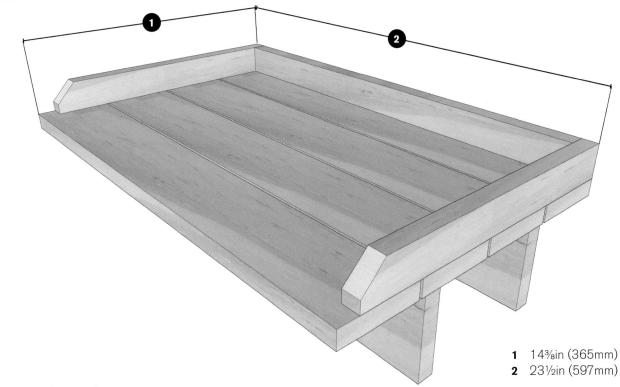

1 14⅜in (365mm)
2 23½in (597mm)

1 13½in (342mm)
2 Cut to fit between side rails
3 1in (25mm)
4 ⅞in (22mm)
5 ½in (12mm)
6 23½in (597mm)
7 3½in (90mm)
8 1½in (38mm)

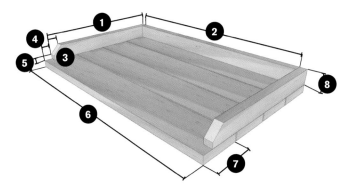

1 Start by cutting the three pieces that form the lip along the upper surface of the tray from ¾ x 1½in (19 x 38mm) stock. They serve as an attachment point for the tray slats. Cut the upper corner of the side piece at 45° as shown. Cut the four slats to length that make up the base of the tray from ¾ x 3½in (19 x 90mm) boards.

2 To start the assembly process, place the pieces that make up the lip upside down on the work surface. Position the rear slat flush with the end of the side lip pieces. Make sure the slat and lip pieces are square before fastening them using 1½in (40mm) screws. Leave about a ⅛in (3mm) gap between them. The front slat will overhang the lip sides.

3 Turn the tray over, then measure and cut a lip piece to fit snugly between the sides.

4 Once more, turn the tray upside down and fasten the rear lip with three screws.

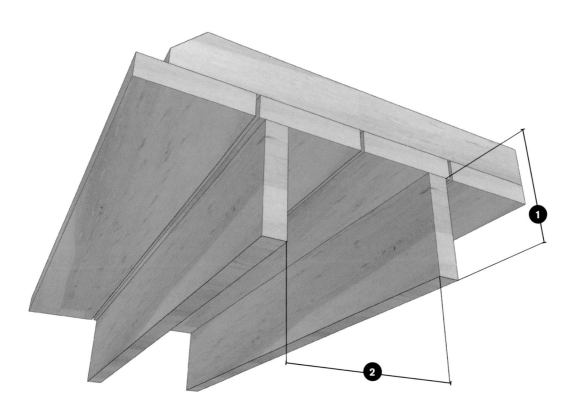

1   3½in (90mm)
2   Space to fit snug over deck rail

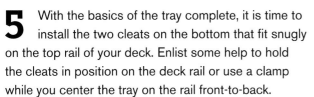

5 With the basics of the tray complete, it is time to install the two cleats on the bottom that fit snugly on the top rail of your deck. Enlist some help to hold the cleats in position on the deck rail or use a clamp while you center the tray on the rail front-to-back.

6 Finally, mark the location of the cleats on the sides of the tray and use 1½in (40mm) screws to fasten the tray to the cleats. Having extra space for food, drink, and condiments is always a good thing to have available during a garden party. You'll soon find out how practical it is to have on hand.

Hammock Stand

There's nothing better than relaxing under the shade of a tree with a cool drink and a good book. This standalone hammock stand provides an easy way to sway in the breeze anywhere in your yard. Made of construction lumber, the materials are easy on the wallet and make for a stout assembly.

LUMBER REQUIRED

9 1½ x 3½ x 96in (38 x 90 x 2440mm)

MATERIALS REQUIRED

1lb (454g) #8 x 2½in (4 x 60mm) exterior screws
1lb (454g) #8 x 3in (4 x 80mm) exterior screws
100 #8 x 1¼in (4 x 30mm) wafer-head screws
2 ⁵⁄₁₆ x 5in (8 x 130mm) carriage bolts with flat washers and hex nuts
4 1½ x 6 x 6in (38 x 152 x 152mm) steel L straps
4 1¹³⁄₁₆ x 5in (46 x 127mm) steel tie plates

OVERALL DIMENSIONS

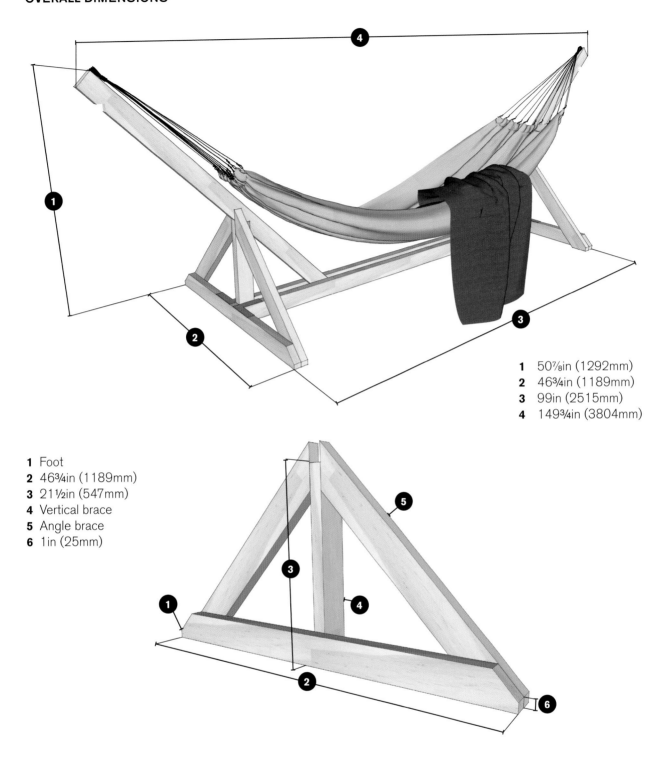

1 50⅞in (1292mm)
2 46¾in (1189mm)
3 99in (2515mm)
4 149¾in (3804mm)

1 Foot
2 46¾in (1189mm)
3 21½in (547mm)
4 Vertical brace
5 Angle brace
6 1in (25mm)

1 Start by building the supporting structures at each end of the hammock stand. Each consists of a horizontal foot, two angle braces, and a vertical brace. They aren't as difficult to build as they appear, but there is one important thing to point out. Making all the 45° cuts is best performed with a circular saw or miter saw. The ultimate stability of the hammock stand relies on the accuracy of these cuts. But don't worry—

it's just a matter of measuring and marking the cut lines accurately. Take your time and follow the steps shown here for the best results. Start by cutting the feet to length and making the 45° cut at each end. Cut the vertical brace next with a 45° cut on one end. The bottom of this brace sits flush with the bottom of the foot as you fasten it to the inside face of the foot.

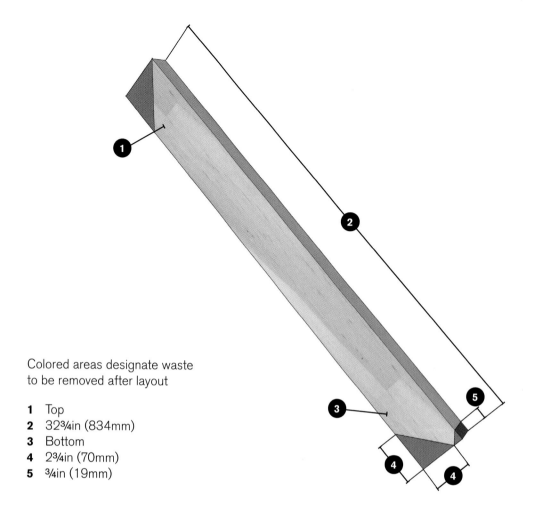

Colored areas designate waste
to be removed after layout

1   Top
2   32¾in (834mm)
3   Bottom
4   2¾in (70mm)
5   ¾in (19mm)

2 Before starting assembly, cut four angle braces as shown in the illustration. After cutting them to final length it's a good idea to lay out the angled cuts while the ends are still square. Then you can remove the waste with a saw.

> **TIP**
> A sturdy, flat work surface will be a big help during assembly. An extra pair of hands wouldn't hurt, either.

3 Attach the angled braces and vertical brace on the inside face of the foot and temporarily fasten them with a single 3in (80mm) screw so you can adjust them for square later.

4 Making sure the vertical brace is square to the foot, secure the angled braces to the foot with 2½in (60mm) screws.

5 Aim to have the joints at the top of the vertical brace tight, with no gaps. (You don't need to fasten the braces at the top yet.)

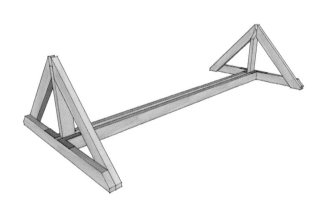

6 On a flat surface, attach the two end assemblies to the pair of 96in (2440mm) boards that form the base. This is a bit tricky, and you'll need some help to hold everything in place as you drive the fasteners. The key is to make sure the vertical brace and foot are square to the base in all directions.

7 Attach the end assembly to the pair of boards that form the base using 3in (80mm) screws from both sides. It's also a good idea to drive a pair of screws from the outside into the end grain of each of the base boards.

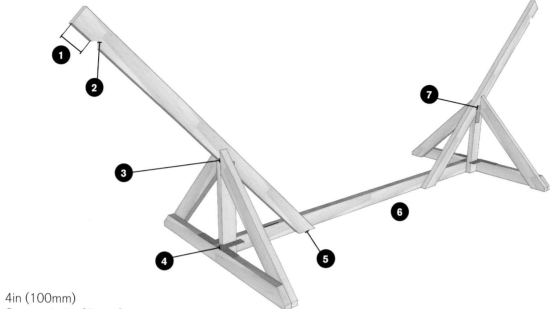

1 4in (100mm)
2 Cut notch 1in (25mm) deep
3 Position bottom of arm along base until joint is tight then fasten arm to base with screws and a carriage bolt, washer, and nut
4 Steel L-strap
5 45° cut
6 Pieces removed to show arms
7 Steel tie plate

8 The final parts to add are the two long, angled arms that support the hammock. After cutting them to length, make the 45° cut on the bottom end of each arm. To prevent the hammock rope from slipping, create a small notch at the top end with a hand saw.

9 When placing the arm in position between the two base boards, have a helper keep an eye on the joint where the arm sits on top of the vertical brace. This is a critical connection, so you'll want to position the arm, so it rests fully and tightly on top of the brace without any gaps. Once that position is locked in, the bottom of the arm should be flush with the bottom of the base. When these conditions are met, you can drive a couple of 3in (80mm) screws from each side of the base to fasten the bottom of the arm.

10 After fastening the bottom of the arm to the base with screws, drill for and install a 5/16 x 5in (8 x 130mm) carriage bolt, washer, and nut. A clamp helps hold all the parts in place as you drill through them.

11 Using #8 x 1¼in (4 x 30mm) wafer-head screws, attach a steel tie plate on both sides of the arm to secure the arm to the top of the vertical brace. Fasten the angled braces using 3in (80mm) screws, keeping the outside face flush with the outside edge of the vertical brace.

12 To beef up the stability of the hammock stand, fasten a pair of steel angle braces at each end to secure the foot to the base. With your favorite hammock in hand, tie it securely to the arms of the stand, making sure the cord at each end is tight in the notch at the top of the arm. Then find yourself a good book, a cool drink, and swing your troubles away.

Storage Bench

Outdoor seating that features a hidden storage bin. This double-duty piece uses a common, hidden storage bin as the basis for the overall design. The lid, or "seat," of the bench is removable to gain access to the bin.

LUMBER REQUIRED

1	¾ x 1½ x 72in (19 x 38 x 1830mm)
7	¾ x 2½ x 72in (19 x 63 x 1830mm)
5	¾ x 3½ x 72in (19 x 90 x 1830mm)
1	1½ x 3½ x 96in (38 x 90 x 2440mm)

MATERIALS REQUIRED

1lb #8 x 1¼in (4 x 30mm) exterior screws
1lb #8 x 1½in (4 x 40mm) exterior screws
1lb #8 x 2in (4 x 50mm) exterior screws

NOTE

Because the size of the storage bin determines the final dimensions of the bench, it's important to have the bin on hand for measurements. The dimensions shown here were designed around the bin that I used (24½L x 17W x 9½inD / 620L x 430W x 240mmD). One other thing to note is that a comfortable seating height is between 15 and 17in (380 and 430mm). So bear this in mind when purchasing the storage bin.

OVERALL DIMENSIONS

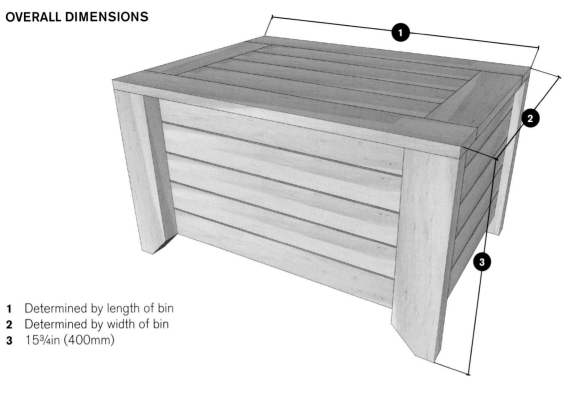

1 Determined by length of bin
2 Determined by width of bin
3 15¾in (400mm)

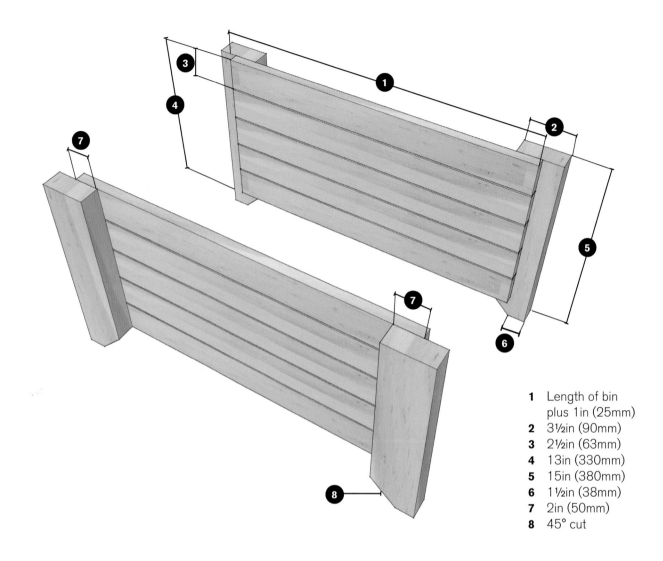

1 Length of bin plus 1in (25mm)
2 3½in (90mm)
3 2½in (63mm)
4 13in (330mm)
5 15in (380mm)
6 1½in (38mm)
7 2in (50mm)
8 45° cut

1 Have the storage bin on hand to determine the final dimensions of the bench.

2 The storage bench is made up of a front and back panel assembly joined by horizontal slats. Start by cutting the legs from a 1½ x 3½in (38 x 90mm) board and making the 45° cut on the bottom end. Cut the slats from ¾ x 2½in (19 x 63mm) boards. Determine which face of each leg has the best appearance and place that face down on the work surface. The angled cuts at the bottom should face each other. The slats overlap the legs by 2in (50mm), so mark a line to serve as a guide when installing the slats. Attach the top and bottom slats first, then space the remaining slats evenly.

3 Mark a guideline on the inside of each leg to align the slats as they are fastened.

4 Fasten the slats to the legs with 1½in (40mm) screws, making sure they are square to the legs and aligned with the guideline you marked on the legs.

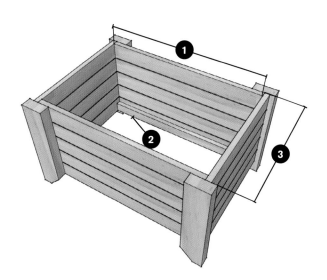

1   Length of bin plus 1in (25mm)
2   Bottom cleat
3   Width of bin plus 1in (25mm)

5 When installing the slats that make up the sides of the bench and connect the front and back assemblies, it's important to try to keep the assembly square. This helps when fitting the lid later. Attach the top slat of each end, then check that the assembly is square. To help with this, use a square at each corner to see what adjustments need to be made. Temporarily attach a brace to hold the assembly square as you install the remaining slats. You may need a helper to hold the assembly square as you fasten the brace.

6 Connect the front and back assemblies with slats cut from ¾ x 2½in (19 x 63mm) boards, aligned with the previously installed slats and fastened with 1½in (40mm) screws.

7 Four widely spaced slats form the bottom of the bench. To hold these slats in place, cut and install a pair of cleats along the bottom inside edge. Install the bottom cleats along the inside bottom edge of the front and back with 1¼in (30mm) screws. After attaching the cleats, flip the box upright and attach the four bottom slats, cut from ¾ x 3½in (19 x 90mm) boards, to the cleats using 1½in (38mm) screws.

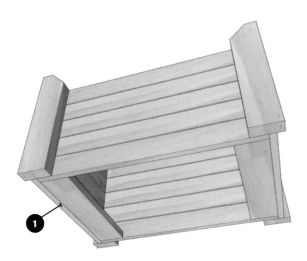

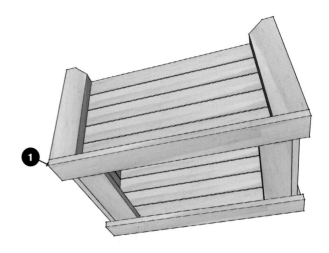

8 The lid of the storage bench is made up of a frame and slats with two cleats underneath that fit the opening of the base, all cut from ¾ x 3½in (19 x 90mm) boards. Before installing the bottom slats, build the lid by first cutting the lid cleats to fit the opening between the front and back. Cut them about ⅛in (3mm) short to make it easier to set the lid in place later. With the base of the bench top-side down on the work surface set the cleats in place.

1 Lid cleats cut ⅛in (3mm) shorter than distance between front and back of bench base

9 Cut the front and back long rails of the lid frame and set them in place under the cleat and base, aligning the outside corners with the corners of the legs.

1 Front and back rails of lid frame, cut to fit flush with outside of legs

10 Align the long pieces of the lid frame with the outside of the legs.

11 An inside view shows the lid frame pieces and cleats in position.

12 To make assembly and placement of the lid components easier, mark the position of the lid frame pieces at all four corners.

13 On the inside of the base, mark the position of the lid cleats on the frame pieces.

14 Lift off the base and secure the cleats to the lid frame rails using 1¼in (30mm) screws.

15 Test the fit of the lid and base.

16 Cut the short pieces that make up the ends of the lid frame to fit between the longer pieces and fasten them with 1¼in (30mm) screws.

NOTE

When fastening the short frame pieces to the cleats, you can fasten them from the bottom side of the lid if you don't want the screws to show. Likewise with the slats that fill in the frame of the lid. It's a matter of personal preference.

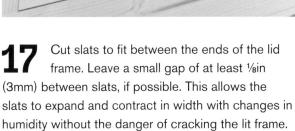

17 Cut slats to fit between the ends of the lid frame. Leave a small gap of at least ⅛in (3mm) between slats, if possible. This allows the slats to expand and contract in width with changes in humidity without the danger of cracking the lit frame.

18 Insert the storage bin and set the lid in place. Having a place to store outdoor accessories yet remain easily accessible can be a challenge. Now you have an attractive solution that no one will suspect unless you show them.

Picnic Table

A traditional picnic table is a must-have for get-togethers with family and friends. This design has been downsized a bit and features an "anti-tipping" base for stable seating. Made almost entirely of construction lumber, it's sure to be a part of many outdoor gatherings.

LUMBER REQUIRED

5 1½ x 3½ x 96in (38 x 90 x 2440mm)

9 1½ x 5½ x 96in (38 x 140 x 2440mm)

1 ¾ x 1½ x 24in (19 x 38 x 610mm)

MATERIALS REQUIRED

1lb (454g) #8 x 2½in (4 x 60mm) exterior screws

1lb (454g) #8 x 3in (4 x 80mm) exterior screws

12 ⁵⁄₁₆ x 4½in (8 x 110mm) carriage bolts, nuts, and washers

OVERALL DIMENSIONS

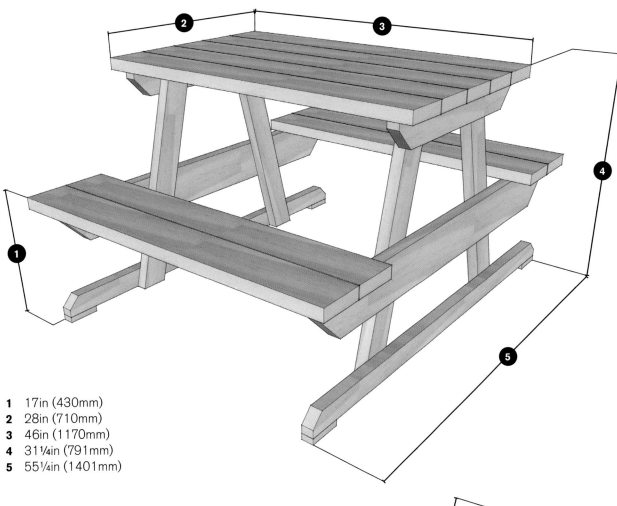

1 17in (430mm)
2 28in (710mm)
3 46in (1170mm)
4 31¼in (791mm)
5 55¼in (1401mm)

1 To build the picnic table, you'll make two end assemblies with each made up of a pair of legs, top support, seat support, and foot. These two assemblies are joined by a stretcher and crowned with planks for the seats and tabletop. Start by cutting the four legs from 1½ x 3½in (38 x 90mm) boards as shown. The areas marked in red show the angles to be cut after the leg is first cut to overall, final length.

Colored areas designate waste to be removed after layout

1 1in (25mm)
2 31in (785mm)
3 9⅝in (246mm)
4 10½in (267mm)
5 Locate bottom of seat support on this line

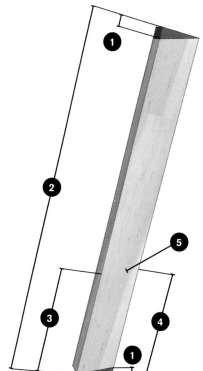

2 To begin assembly, place the legs flat on the work surface and locate the seat support, centering it on the legs and aligned with the locations you marked earlier. Take the time here to measure and mark lines for the location of the seat support. Cut the seat supports to length from 1½ x 5½in (38 x 140mm) boards, then make the 45° cut at each end on the bottom edge. Install only one 2½in (60mm) screw at each joint where the seat support crosses the legs. This allows you to pivot the legs to align the bottoms flat on the work surface. Then you can add an additional screw to secure the seat support to the legs.

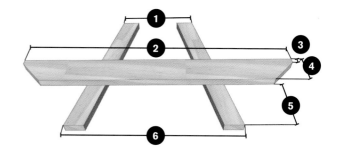

1 16⅜in (415mm)
2 55¼in (1401mm)
3 1in (25mm)
4 5½in (140mm)
5 9¼in (235mm)
6 32in (815mm)

3 After attaching the seat support to the legs with only one screw, enlist a helper to stand the assembly up on a flat surface to ensure the bottom of the legs sit flat. Then insert an additional screw to lock the seat support in place.

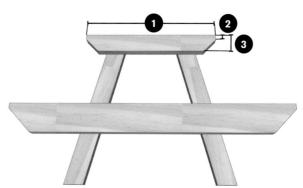

4 Cut the two top supports to length from 1½ x 3½in (38 x 90mm) stock and make the 45° angled cuts on the bottom corners.

1 26⅜in (670mm)
2 1in (25mm)
3 3½in (90mm)

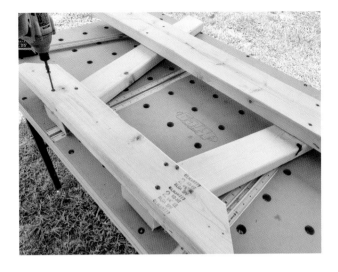

5 Center the top support on the legs, flush with the top of the legs, and secure it with 2½in (60mm) screws.

1 39in (990mm)

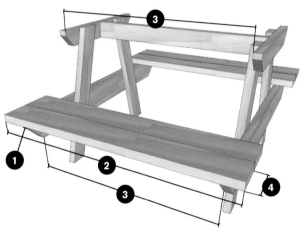

6 Stand the two end assemblies top-down on a flat surface. Cut the stretcher to length from a 1½ x 3½in (38 x 90mm) board and secure it with 3in (80mm) screws, making sure it's square to the end assemblies.

7 Enlist an extra pair of hands to flip the assembly right-side up on a flat surface. Cut the planks for the top and seats from 1½ x 5½in (38 x 140mm) boards. Before fastening them to the supports, measure the distance between the leg assemblies at the top and bottom. This helps ensure the assembly is square when fastening the planks. Check this dimension frequently as you attach the planks.

1 1½in (38mm) overhang
2 46in (1170mm)
3 39in (990mm)
4 5½in (140mm)

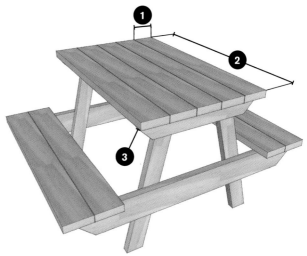

8 Install the seat planks with 3in (80mm) screws. Offset the outside screw on the outer plank so that the screw doesn't protrude through the angled cut in the seat support. Leave at least ⅛in (3mm) space between the planks.

1 5½in (140mm)
2 46in (1170mm)
3 1in (25mm) overhang

9 Attach the center plank for the top first, using 3in (80mm) screws.

10 Use 3in (80mm) screws as spacers to position the remaining planks.

11 Locate the outer screws to avoid the screw exiting at the angled cut in the top support.

12 The table looks complete, but to add stability, add a foot at each end of the table cut to length from 1½ x 3½in (38 x 90mm) boards.

1   3½in (90mm)
2   4in (100mm)
3   55¼in (1401mm)

13 Flip the table on its end to make it easy to attach the foot.

14 To further strengthen the assembly, drill ⁵⁄₁₆in (8mm) holes at all the joints and install carriage bolts with a washer and nut. Install two bolts each where the seat support attaches to the legs.

15 Attach a pad cut to length from a ¾ x 1½in (19 x 38mm) board at each end of the foot using 1½in (40mm) screws.

16 With foot and pads in place and all the carriage bolts installed, flip the table to the opposite end and repeat the process. The picnic table is sure to be a hot spot for food and conversation at your next party.

Swing

An old-fashioned porch swing invites young and old alike to sit and relax. The gentle back-and-forth motion has a soothing, almost hypnotic effect. The swing is made up of a seat frame with a vertical support at each corner. An arm connects the tops of the supports at each end. A seatback frame connects to the seat frame and arm assembly. Finish it off with slats on the seat and back, add the hardware for a hanging chain, and you'll soon be able to lull yourself to sleep.

LUMBER REQUIRED

3 ¾ x 1½ x 72in (19 x 38 x 1830mm)

4 ¾ x 2½ x 72in (19 x 63 x 1830mm)

5 ¾ x 3½ x 72in (19 x 90 x 1830mm)

1 ¾ x 5½ x 72in (19 x 140 x 1830mm)

1 1½ x 3½ x 96in (38 x 90 x 2440mm)

MATERIALS REQUIRED

1lb (454g) #8 x 1½in (4 x 40mm) exterior screws

1lb (454g) #8 x 2in (4 x 50mm) exterior screws

4   ⁵⁄₁₆ x 5in (8 x 130mm) eyebolts

Porch swing kit with chains and S-hooks

OVERALL DIMENSIONS

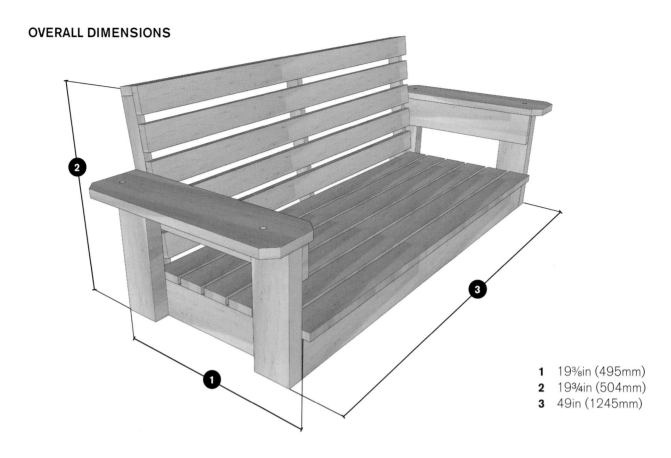

1   19⅜in (495mm)
2   19¾in (504mm)
3   49in (1245mm)

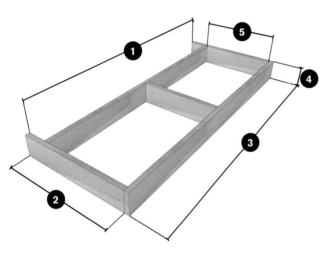

1 Start by building the seat frame. It serves as the foundation for the rest of the swing assembly.

1   44½in (1132mm)
2   17⅞in (452mm)
3   46in (1170mm)
4   3½in (90mm)
5   14in (355mm)

2 After cutting the pieces for the seat frame to length from ¾ x 3½in (19 x 90mm) stock, fasten them with 2in (50mm) screws. Center the internal divider between the ends of the frame.

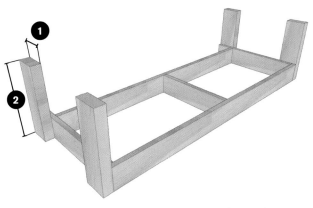

1   3½in (90mm)
2   11⅝in (296mm)

3 Cut the four vertical posts to length from 1½ x 3½in (38 x 90mm) boards. Fasten them to the outside of the seat frame with 2in (50mm) screws. Make sure the posts are square to the frame and flush with the front and back edges of the frame.

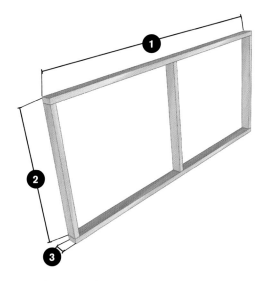

1   44½in (1132mm)
2   17¾in (449mm)
3   1½in (38mm)

4 To make the frame for the seatback, cut the spars from ¾ x 1½in (19 x 38mm) stock. Follow the same process and use the same size of screws as you did for the seat frame.

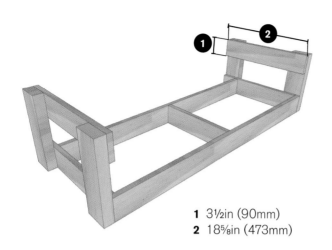

1 3½in (90mm)
2 18⅝in (473mm)

5 Cut the arm supports from ¾ x 3½in (19 x 90mm) stock. Fasten them to the inside face of the vertical supports using 2in (50mm) screws.

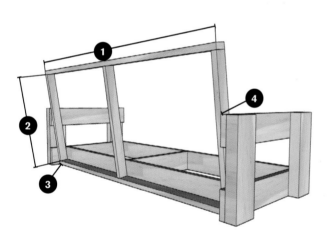

6 The back frame connects to the inside face of the seat frame at the back. It also connects to the arm support. The back frame fits tight against the back rail of the seat frame with the sides of the back frame aligned with the back corner of the arm support.

1 44½in (1132mm)
2 17¾in (449mm)
3 Back frame flush with bottom of seat frame
4 Back frame aligned with upper corner of arm brace

7 The swing hangs by chains connected to eyebolts at each corner of the seat frame. To create a solid seatback, make sure to locate and drill the ⁵⁄₁₆in (8mm) hole for the eyebolt at the bottom of the seatback so that it passes close to the center of the frame side.

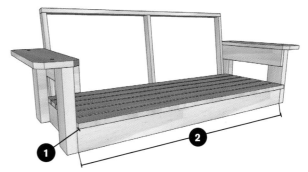

1   ¾in (19mm) overhang
2   Cut slats to fit flush with ends of seat frame. All
    slats are cut from ¾ x 2½in (19 x 63mm) stock.

8 Drill a ⁵⁄₁₆in (8mm) hole centered on the widths of the vertical post and seat frame. Install an eyebolt vertically, as shown, and fasten it tight with a washer and then a nut.

TIP

The eyebolt at the bottom of the seatback frame passes close to the midpoint of the frame side. This hole through the seatback frame, seat frame, and vertical post might be easiest to drill from the inside.

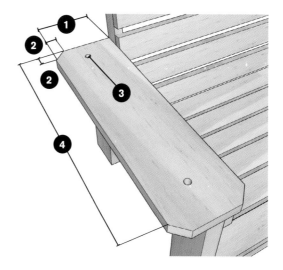

9 Install the front slat with a ¾in (19mm) overhang. A scrap piece serves as a handy guide. Attach the rear slat tight to the seatback frame then space the remaining slats evenly.

1   5½in (140mm)
2   1in (25mm)
3   ¾in (19mm)-dia.
4   19¾in (504mm)

NOTE

Attach the arms (see step 10) before drilling the holes for the chains to pass through (see step 15).

10 Cut the arms from ¾ x 5½ (19 x 140mm) stock. Before drilling the holes where the chains will pass through, fasten the arms using 2in (50mm) screws, aligning the inside edge flush with the arm support.

11 Align the seatback frame with the upper corner of the arm, drill a ⁵⁄₁₆in (8mm) hole centered on the frame and arm support, then install a carriage bolt, washer, and nut.

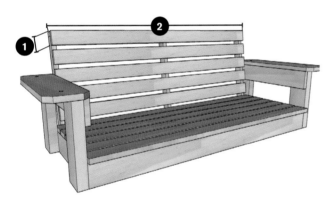

1 2½in (63mm)
2 Cut slats to fit flush with ends of back frame.
All slats are cut from ¾ x 2½in (19 x 63mm) stock.

12 When installing the back slats, space the bottom slat ¾in (19mm) from the seat and make the top slat flush with the top of the seatback frame. Space the remaining slats evenly.

13 The chains for the swing connect to the eyebolts with S-hooks and pass through holes in the arms. These holes need to be aligned with the center of the eyebolts. Measure and make note of the horizontal position of the eyebolts by referencing the tape measure from the back of the rear post. Transfer these measurements to the top of the arm. Measure from the inside of the arm support to the center of the eyebolt and transfer these locations to the top of the arm.

14 After determining where to locate the pair of holes in each arm so they align with the eyebolts below, drill ¾in (19mm) holes.

15 Pass the chains through the holes in the arms.

16 Connect an S-hook between the eyebolt and chain. When it comes time to hang the swing, you have a few options. You can build or purchase a standalone swing frame for your yard. Or you can mount the swing to the ceiling of a porch. In either case, make sure the method and fasteners used to hang the swing can support the full weight of the swing and occupants. If there is any doubt about a safe installation, contact a licensed contractor to give you a hand. All that's left to do now is grab a few throw pillows, kick off your shoes, and let the gentle motion of the swing transport you to a peaceful place.

Adirondack Chair

This style of outdoor chair has been around for decades, and for good reason. It's so comfortable to sit in that you never want to get up. At first glance, you might think that building this chair would be anything but simple. But all you need to do is take one step at a time and you'll end up with a chair that will soon become a favorite.

LUMBER REQUIRED

2 ¾ x 2½ x 72in (19 x 63 x 1830mm)

6 ¾ x 3½ x 72in (19 x 90 x 1830mm)

2 ¾ x 5½ x 72in (19 x 140 x 1830mm)

2 1½ x 3½ x 96in (38 x 90 x 2440mm)

MATERIALS REQUIRED

1lb (454g) #8 x 1¼in (4 x 30mm) exterior screws

1lb (454g) #8 x 1½in (4 x 40mm) exterior screws

1lb (454g) #8 x 2in (4 x 50mm) exterior screws

1lb (454g) #8 x 3in (4 x 76mm) exterior screws

4 ⁵⁄₁₆ x 2in (8 x 50mm) carriage bolts with flat washers and hex nuts

4 ⁵⁄₁₆ x 3in (8 x 76mm) carriage bolts with flat washers and hex nuts

2 ⁵⁄₁₆ x 4in (8 x 102mm) carriage bolts with flat washers and hex nuts

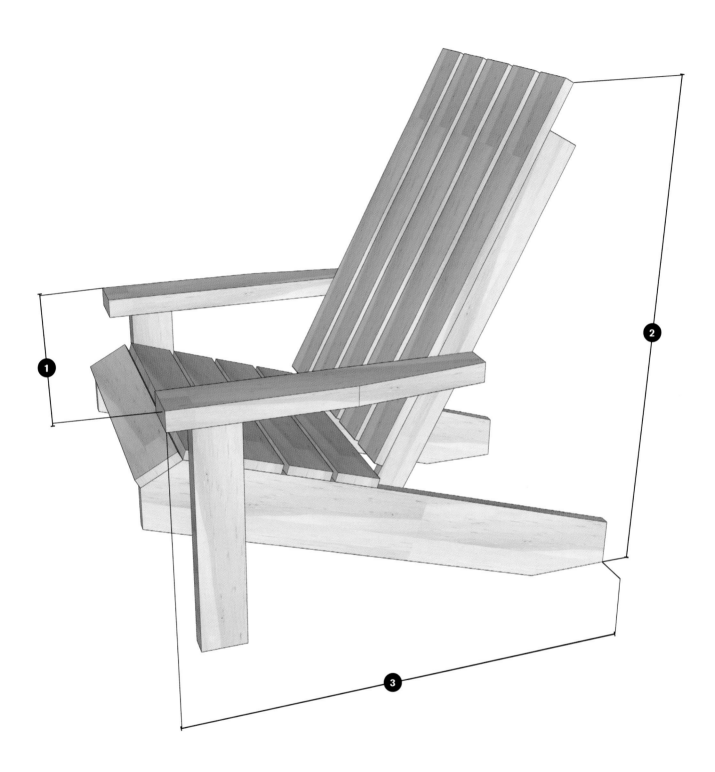

1 27½in (697mm)
2 38⅜in (975mm)
3 36⅞in (937mm)

OUTSIDE FACE OF SIDE RAIL   INSIDE FACE OF SIDE RAIL

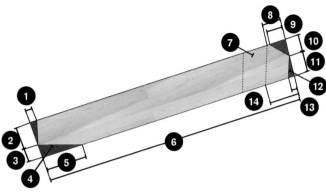

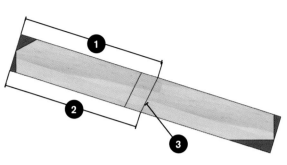

1 21⅜in (545mm)
2 20⅜in (520mm)
3 Slope for rear of seatback

Colored areas designate waste
to be removed after layout

1 1⅛in (30mm)   **8** 2⅞in (72mm)
2 3½in (90mm)   **9** 2½in (63mm)
3 2in (50mm)   **10** 2½in (63mm)
4 Bottom   **11** 3in (75mm)
5 6½in (165mm)   **12** Front
6 40½in (1027mm)   **13** ⅞in (22mm)
7 Location of front leg **14** 4⅝in (116mm)

1 The most challenging part of building the chair is cutting the two angled side rails to shape. The easiest way to accomplish this is to start by cutting them to final length (40½in/1027mm) from ¾ x 5½in (19 x 140mm) boards. On the outside face of the rail, mark the location of the front leg. On the inside face of the rail, mark the location for the seatback. Remember that the two side rails are mirror images of each other. Lay out and mark all the cuts to remove the waste (shown in red).

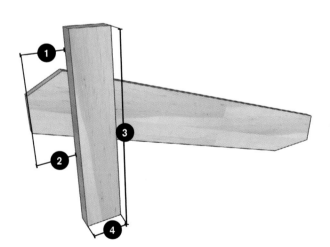

1 3½in (90mm)
2 3½in (90mm)
3 18in (460mm)
4 3½in (90mm)

2 Cut the pair of front legs from a 1½ x 3½ (38 x 90mm) board. With the front leg positioned at the location you marked earlier on the side rail, fasten the side rail to the leg with a single 2in (50mm) screw.

3 Make sure the bottom edge of the side rail and bottom of the front leg are flat to the work surface then drive a second screw to secure the rail to the leg.

4 With the two leg assemblies complete, you can turn your attention to making the frame for the seatback.

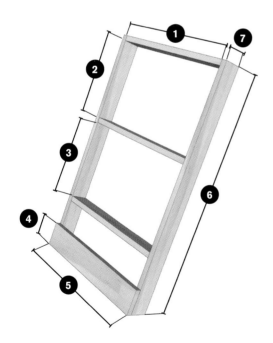

1 19in (485mm)
2 11⅝in (296mm)
3 11⅝in (296mm)
4 3½in (90mm)
5 20½in (522mm)
6 33⅛in (843mm)
7 2½in (63mm)

5 Assemble the frame for the seat back using 2in (50mm) screws, making sure everything is square as you go.

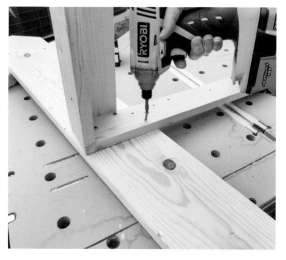

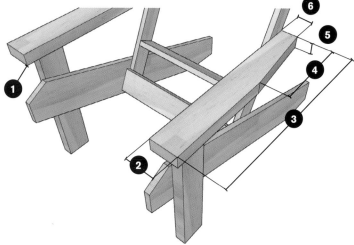

6 Using the guidelines you made earlier before cutting the side rails, locate the seatback frame and fasten it with 1¼in (30mm) screws. With some assistance from a friend, attach the opposite leg assembly in the same manner. To provide an upper anchor point for the back frame, make the arms next.

1 2in (50mm) overhang
2 3½in (90mm)
3 23¾in (604mm)
4 10¼in (261mm)
5 1½in (38mm)
6 2¼in (55mm)

7 Locate the arms to the tops of the front legs with a ¾in (19mm) overhang on the inside and a 2in (50mm) overhang at the front end of the arm. Drive a 3in (80mm) screw to fasten the arm to the front leg.

8 Temporarily fasten the seatback frame to the back end of the arm with 2in (50mm) screws until you fasten the seat slats.

9 Drill a ⁵⁄₁₆in (8mm) hole through the seatback frame and arm then install a 4in (100mm) carriage bolt.

10 Add a washer then a nut but leave the joint loose for now.

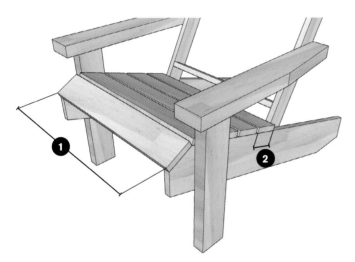

1 22in (560mm)
2 3½in (90mm)

11 Cut the seat slats from ¾ x 3½in (19 x 90 mm) boards. Install them using 1½in (40mm) screws. You may have to move the arm out of the way for easier access. Align the front slat with the angled cut at the front. Fit the rear slat tight against the seatback frame. Space the remaining slats evenly.

12 Tighten the carriage bolt that secures the arm and use a couple of 3in (80mm) screws to make the final attachment to the front leg. Refer to illustration on the right for the proper positioning of the arm relative to the front leg.

13 Drill and install a pair of 3in (80mm) carriage bolts through the front legs and rear frame to secure them to the side rail.

14 Secure the back to the side rail with carriage bolts, washers, and nuts.

15 The last items to add are the vertical slats for the seatback, which are cut from ¾ x 3½in (19 x 90 mm) boards. Start with the two outside slats, then the center slat. Space the remaining two slats evenly. Install the slats with 1½in (40mm) screws, spacing them ¾in (19mm) above the seat slats. It's a sure bet that no matter where you place this chair, you'll soon have folks scrambling to be the first to sit in it. When it's finally your turn, you can settle back with a cold beverage and soak up the sun.

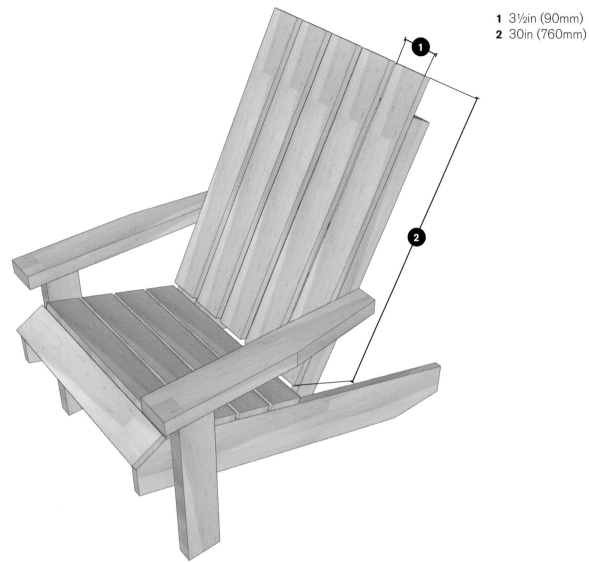

1 3½in (90mm)
2 30in (760mm)

About the Author

Randall (Randy) Maxey is a full-time author, editor, and woodworker. His late father, Riley, was a woodworker and handyman and was a role model of how to "do it right the first time."

Randall produces print, web, and video content for several woodworking publications and tool manufacturers. His previous books include: *Sharpening, A Woodworker's Guide*; *Woodworking Basics*; and *Outdoor Woodworking Games*, all published by GMC Publications.

When he's not in the workshop or busy at his keyboard, Randy likes to go "hunting" with his camera on nature trails. And, yes, during the Christmas holiday season, he portrays Santa Claus.

Randy resides in Florida with his wife Sheryl.

DEDICATION

This book is dedicated to my late father, Riley Maxey. Every time I pick up a tool, I think of you, Dad. Thanks for teaching me the importance of doing good work.

ACKNOWLEDGMENTS

Writing a book is a process. For this book, it started with an idea, then progressed to an outline; project design; building the projects while documenting each build with photos and illustrations; draft submittal; and edits. Along the way, there are many people involved in each of those steps.

My gratitude first goes to my wife, Sheryl, who was my hand model, nurse, mental health counsellor, and cheerleader. She put up with sawdust being tracked into our home. She was most patient as our living room became a storage area for tools, lumber, and projects in various stages of completion. She tried her best to keep me sane during the long, hot days of building and countless hours of generating illustrations, organizing photos, and writing.

My son, Aaron, was a big help in moving projects around and loading them up for transport. He also filled in as a hand model on one of the projects. Thanks, Son!

To my friends, Bruce and Candie Thornton, who assisted in building the garden bridge as a "trial run" for creating the rest of the projects. Your friendship is dear to me.

Building outdoor projects in the middle of summer in the southeastern United States is a hot proposition.

Our friends Scott and Stephanie Smith were gracious enough to loan their tent canopy to help shield us from the sun.

My good friend, Alan Goodsell, was also a great encouragement and a much-appreciated liaison between the publisher and me. Alan allowed me to bounce design ideas off him and provided creative insights. He also provided temporary storage for the projects and was the chief photographer for the main project photos.

I'm sure I've caused more than a few headaches for the folks at GMC Publications in the UK: Jonathan Bailey, Wendy McAngus, Emma Foster, and Dominique Page. They were responsible for trying to keep me on track and on schedule, which proved to be rather difficult. And they are the ones that put the spit and polish on my rough submissions to create the book you are holding in your hands. Thanks to you all.

Many thanks to Dan and Romina Diaco for letting us use their delightful garden as a location for our outdoor photography.

But most of all, thank you, reader, for purchasing this book. I couldn't do this without your interest and support.

Index

First published 2022 by
Guild of Master Craftsman Publications Ltd
Castle Place, 166 High Street, Lewes,
East Sussex BN7 1XU

Text © Randall Maxey, 2022
Copyright in the Work © GMC Publications Ltd, 2022

ISBN 978 1 78494 620 3

A catalog record for this book is available from the
British Library.

Publisher Jonathan Bailey
Production Director Jim Bulley
Senior Project Editor Dominique Page
Managing Art Editor Robin Shields
Designer Rhiann Bull
Photographers Randall Maxey & Alan Goodsell

Colour origination by GMC Reprographics
Printed and bound in Malaysia

To place an order, contact:

GMC PUBLICATIONS LTD
Castle Place, 166 High Street,
Lewes, East Sussex,
BN7 1XU
United Kingdom
Tel: +44 (0)1273 488005
www.gmcbooks.com